D1014760

Why Learn From Small Towns? What Business People Are Saying...

"Only in a small town can you discover the true nature of what it means to be connected and, at the same time, living in a fish bowl."

—**Tim Sanders, NY Times Bestselling Author,** *Love Is the Killer App*

"People say the world is getting smaller; I think the world is getting more connected. It's all about the relationships—who you know and who knows you. Through the power of the Internet, mobile apps, and online social networking platforms like Facebook, Twitter, Google+, and LinkedIn, businesses now have unprecedented ways in which to nurture relationships with everyone in their marketplace. We're going back to the small town way of doing business where everyone knows your name and genuinely cares about you."

—**Mari Smith, Author,** *The New Relationship Marketing*

"For generations, small town businesses have been responsible for building the American economy, and all entrepreneurs can learn a thing or two from their success."

—**Scott Gerber, Founder, Young Entrepreneur Council; Cofounder, Gen Y Capital Partners; Author,** *Never Get a "Real" Job*

"Small town businesses *know* their customers. They know their kids' names, they know their favorite sports teams, and what they buy on a regular basis. This kind of intimate knowledge creates loyalty—the kind of loyalty that creates longevity and success in business."

—**Carol Roth, NY Times Bestselling Author,** *The Entrepreneur Equation*

"Small is the new big, because you can reach everyone with the click of a mouse and anyone can review and critique you. Think you know how to play the game? Think again. The rules have changed. Read *Small Town Rules*. It's the rule book for the connected economy. Highly recommended."

—**Michael Port, NY Times Bestselling Author,** *Book Yourself Solid*

"Business should be personal. The 'who you are' can play a huge role in the 'what you offer.' That's how small towns have conducted commerce since the get-go, and we'd all be well-served to inject that kind of approach to our businesses—no matter how big in scope or vision."

—**Rich Sloan, Author,** *StartUp Nation*

"There are a lot of traits about small town business that offer insights and opportunities for people to leverage in all businesses. Community matters. Relationships matter. People matter.

My observation about conversations in a small town is that people care. And businesses that are smart are learning to listen, connect, share, and engage their customers, too. Big business and businesses in general could learn a lot from how a small town works."

—Jeff Pulver, Cofounder, Vonage; Founder,
140 Characters Conference, VON Conference

"In a small town, word of mouth is the most powerful force there is. Everyone in town knows about the business. If the quality and service are good—or bad—everyone soon knows. That's why every business should operate like a small town business, no matter where you're located or how far away your customers come from. When you and your team run your business as if every potential customer will eventually know everything about your business, you naturally will keep quality and service standards high."

—Anita Campbell, CEO, Small Business Trends, LLC;
Author, *Visual Marketing*

"It is no surprise that big businesses are coming around to the idea of small town style customer experience and service. As customers, we know we prefer the 'small town' way of doing things. We like to be treated as human beings, as individuals. We like our loyalty being rewarded, and we like having a person to talk to when things go wrong. When it comes across as natural, rather than forced in an awkwardly fake 'PR' way, then it works all the better. The future of business is one customer at a time, just like in small town businesses."

—Chris Garrett, Coauthor, *ProBlogger: The Book*

"Small town businesses, by their nature, are genetically encoded to connect, share, and engage."

—Alan Weinkrantz, Alan Weinkrantz and Company PR

"With a couple of basic tools, like DropBox, Skype, and Google Apps, a small town business can look like a big business with one killer app: You can stay in a small town with the associated lifestyle benefits and lower cost of doing business. Small town businesses are rewriting the rules on what it means to be competitive with their big company rivals for customers and talented employees."

—John Warrillow, Author, *Built to Sell*

"Small town businesses understand this better than most any publicly traded company in the world: You must be cash flow positive or it's your death. As long as you have positive cash flow, you can keep the doors open, expand as much as your cash flow will let you, and try new things. Big businesses are accustomed to running deficits and issuing stock, but these are stopgap measures that more often than not serve to enrich the shareholders as the ship sinks. If your business, big or small, is cash flow positive, then everyone from shareholders to shop floor sweepers will do well."

—Christopher S. Penn, Vice President of Strategy and Innovation at Blue Sky Factory Email Marketing

"A key to success for any small business is to be actively involved in their community. That feeling of 'community' is what drives the web and social media. Now, it's just about mandatory that businesses of all sizes be active in their respective communities—both online and off. It's the interaction, the connection with those who support you, that helps make businesses successful today."

—Leslie McLellan, All Things Social

"During the past four decades, big has gotten the attention in my industry sector. Economies of scale, resources for impressive events. But, what's becoming clear is that the relationships, the personal attention, the value of doing life together is what matters. I know. I'm a pastor, not a business owner. But, the ideas that Becky and Barry are talking about for what small businesses can teach all business is true in our 'business.' While big churches get the press, the number of house churches, of communities of faith, is growing, too. Small, done well, can teach all of us how to live and work better."

—Jon Swanson, Social Media Chaplain

"Small town business has to do with the basics. Those simpler times that city-dwellers dream about when they're sitting in a 2-hour traffic jam, listening to their satellite radio, while pounding out meaningless emails and texts on heavily used Blackberrys. Small town businesses are a lot more about handshakes than they are about 14-page contracts that Harvard Law School graduates write…and that no one ever seems to understand. All business owners can learn a lot by watching how business gets done in America's small towns."

—Joel Libava, The Franchise King®; Author, *Become a Franchise Owner!*

"Although the competitiveness of large population areas (between individual businesses) might be tougher, it does not compare to the daily fight for survival in a small town or remote area. This fight for survival brings out the best of entrepreneurial spirit in many small town businesses with innovation, service, and quality. The real treasure of small town business is the heart! Small town businesses are not just serving strangers, but their neighbors, friends, family, or someone who knows these people who are important to them. This natural sincerity that comes from living in small communities can be duplicated in practice by all business, and I believe it is the most valuable asset small business has to share."

—Laura Girty, NW Field Representative, Rural Enterprises of Oklahoma, Inc.

"Small town business can teach all businesses about efficiency. Small businesses don't have the luxury of compartmentalizing roles. It's all hands on deck, working as quickly and seamlessly as possible, to ensure the greatest profit."

—**Alexandra Levit, Author,** *Blind Spots: The 10 Business Myths You Can't Afford to Believe on Your New Path to Success*

"Small town business teaches us that it's easier to continue to sell to the customer we already know. It's easy—just provide great value and consistent quality, and you'll make customers for life."

—**Jim F. Kukral, DigitalBookLaunch.com; Author,** *Attention: This Book Will Make You Money*

"There are more successful small town businesses than there are large corporations. They aren't a fluke or an accident or an anomaly. They grow from need, vision, risk, and response. The information small town business owners offer is practical, tested, and shared generously. Small town business can be easily underestimated but should never be ignored."

—**Andrea Springer, Springer Coaching and Consulting**

"Transparency is the over-used buzzword in the customer-service world of today, thanks to the communication onslaught brought on by the Internet and specifically social media. Due to the 'everyone knows everyone' effect of small towns, small town businesses were forced to become masters of transparency a hundred years earlier than the rest of the world."

—**Cody Heitschmidt, Small Town Business Owner**

"Small town businesses are lean and mean, which means they have to be creative and innovative to compete and turn a profit. Businesses of all sizes can watch and learn in order to do the same."

—**Gini Dietrich, CEO, Arment-Dietrich; SpinSucks.com; Coauthor,** *Marketing in the Round: Multichannel Approaches in the Post-Social Media Era*

"Small town business teaches us about community, trust, and relationship—all the current buzzwords that have been the backbone of small town business for more than 100 years."

—**Sarah Robinson, Escaping Mediocrity**

"A small town business owner knows that every customer is important and that every customer, employee, vendor, partner, friend, and family member contributes to what makes the business grow. Small town businesses know that relationships and being part of the community are at the heart of every successful business and that a business without a heart won't survive."

—**Liz Strauss, International Business Strategist; Author,** *The Secret to Writing a Successful Outstanding Blog;* **Successful-Blog.com**

Small Town Rules

How Big Brands and Small Businesses Can Prosper in a Connected Economy

BARRY J. MOLTZ
BECKY McCRAY

800 East 96th Street,
Indianapolis, Indiana 46240 USA

Small Town Rules: How Big Brands and Small Businesses Can
Prosper in a Connected Economy

Copyright © 2012 by Pearson Education, Inc.

All rights reserved. No part of this book shall be reproduced, stored in
a retrieval system, or transmitted by any means, electronic, mechanical, photocopying, recording, or otherwise, without written permission from the publisher. No patent liability is assumed with respect to
the use of the information contained herein. Although every precau-
tion has been taken in the preparation of this book, the publisher and
author assume no responsibility for errors or omissions. Nor is any
liability assumed for damages resulting from the use of the information contained herein.

ISBN-13: 978-0-7897-4920-8
ISBN-10: 0-7897-4920-3

The Library of Congress cataloging-in-publication data is on file.

Printed in the United States of America

First Printing: April 2012

Trademarks

All terms mentioned in this book that are known to be trademarks
or service marks have been appropriately capitalized. Que Publishing
cannot attest to the accuracy of this information. Use of a term in this
book should not be regarded as affecting the validity of any trademark
or service mark.

Warning and Disclaimer

Every effort has been made to make this book as complete and as
accurate as possible, but no warranty or fitness is implied. The information provided is on an "as is" basis. The authors and the publisher
shall have neither liability nor responsibility to any person or entity
with respect to any loss or damages arising from the information contained in this book.

Bulk Sales

Que Publishing offers excellent discounts on this book when ordered
in quantity for bulk purchases or special sales. For more information,
please contact

U.S. Corporate and Government Sales
1-800-382-3419
corpsales@pearsontechgroup.com

For sales outside of the U.S., please contact

International Sales
international@pearsoned.com

Editor-in-Chief
Greg Wiegand

Senior Acquisitions Editor
Katherine Bull

Development Editor
Ginny Bess Munroe

Managing Editor
Kristy Hart

Project Editor
Jovana San Nicolas-Shirley

Copy Editor
Sheri Cain

Indexer
Lisa Stumpf

Proofreader
Seth Kerney

Technical Editors
Aliza Sherman Risdahl
Britt Raybould

Publishing Coordinators
Cindy Teeters
Romny French

Cover Designer
Anne Jones

Compositor
Nonie Ratcliff

**Que Biz-Tech Editorial
Board**
Michael Brito
Jason Falls
Rebecca Lieb
Simon Salt
Peter Shankman

TABLE OF CONTENTS

About the Authors

Barry J. Moltz grew up in a small town of 30,000 and moved to the third-biggest city in America. Becky McCray grew up in towns ranging from 1,500 to 350,000 and now lives in a tiny town of just 30 people. Both are small business owners.

Barry Moltz gets small business owners unstuck by unlocking their long-forgotten potential. With decades of entrepreneurial experience in his own businesses ventures, as well as consulting countless companies, Barry has discovered the formula to get stuck business owners going again.

Barry has founded and run small businesses with a great deal of success and failure for more than 15 years. After successfully selling his last business, Barry branched out into numerous entrepreneurship-related activities. He founded an angel investor group, an angel fund, and is a former advisory member on the board of the Angel Capital Education Foundation.

His first book, *You Need to Be A Little Crazy: The Truth about Starting and Growing Your Business*, describes the ups and downs and emotional trials of running a business. It is in its fifth reprint and has been translated into Chinese, Russian, Korean, and Thai. His second book, *Bounce! Failure, Resiliency, and the Confidence to Achieve Your Next Great Success*, shows what it takes to come back and develop true business confidence. It has been translated into Korean and German. His third book, *BAM! Delivering Customer Service in a Self-Service World*, shows how customer service is the new marketing.

Barry is a nationally recognized expert on entrepreneurship and has given hundreds of presentations to audiences ranging from 20 to 20,000 people. As a member of the Entrepreneurship Hall of Fame, he also has taught entrepreneurship as an adjunct professor at the Illinois Institute of Technology. Barry has appeared on many TV and radio programs, such as *The Big Idea* with Donny Deutsch, MSNBC's *Your Business* and *The Tavis Smiley Show*. He hosts his own radio show, *Business Insanity Talk Radio*. He blogs regularly for the American Express Open Forum and Crain's *Chicago Business*.

Becky McCray has been called "the small town Seth Godin" for her savvy combination of rural entrepreneurship and marketing skills. She started her first business venture in junior high school and has been going ever since. Currently, she and her husband own and operate a cattle ranch and a retail liquor store. Along with Sheila Scarborough, she co-founded Tourism Currents to teach tourism professionals new marketing skills. Like many rural entrepreneurs, she has pieced together multiple lines of business to build a career.

Becky is a recognized expert in small business and social media and has taught nearly 1,000 classroom hours and more than 100 workshops and speeches on small business subjects. She has been featured in *The New York Times, BusinessWeek, Inc., Entrepreneur, Niche, Winning Workplaces, Reimagine Rural, Community Developer*, and the *Agurban*. Becky publishes one of the top 20 small business blogs in the world, Small Biz Survival, which is focused on small town small business.

What makes all this possible is her wide experience in small town business, community, and government. That includes work as a small town administrator, a non-profit executive with the local workforce development and Girl Scout councils, an antiques store owner, a business and computer consultant, and a newspaper reporter. For nine years, McCray spent her evenings and weekends teaching a variety of computer and business classes at local technology centers, making her the fourth generation of her family to teach. In 2004, she was an unsuccessful candidate for the Oklahoma House of Representatives. She believes we learn from both our successes and our failures, even when those failures are printed in the local newspaper.

Dedication

From Barry:
To my parents, Alan and Carole Moltz, who fortunately brought me up in a small town.

From Becky:
To my long-suffering husband, Joe, who misses me when I'm gone.

Acknowledgments

From Barry:

Thank you to my coauthor, Becky McCray, who is not only the inspiration for this book, but a perfect example of using small town rules to be a successful business owner.

Sara, Ethan, and Daniel, who allow me to work "anywhere, anywhen."

Jun Shihan Nancy Lanoue and Kyoshi Sarah Ludden, my Seido Karate teachers at Thousand Waves, who taught me what it really means to be part of a thriving community.

Tracy Thirion, the most creative person I know.

Mike Cooper, my father-in-law, may he rest in peace, who knew how to be successful while planning for zero.

From Becky:

Barry Moltz, thank you for knowing that small towns don't mean small time and for asking all the right questions to make this a better book.

Glenna Mae Hendricks, my mom, thank you for letting me tag along on your small town entrepreneurial adventures from an early age.

Jon Swanson, thank you. (Jon will just say, "whatever.")

Sheila Scarborough, thanks for putting up with me.

Thank you to my online mastermind friends who listened and encouraged as I worked on this idea for several years: Erno Hannink, Pieter van Osch, Stephanie Ward, Paul Merrill, Glenda Watson Hyatt, Deb Brown, Rick Mahn, and Todd Jordan.

Thank you to my first bloggy friend, Chris. What an adventure this has all turned out to be, eh?

Laurie Reyes, thank you for helping with this book and keeping everything else going while we worked on it.

Thanks to my dad, the late Charles Allen, who used his small town business sense to go a long way.

From Both Barry and Becky:

Thanks to Katherine Bull, our acquisition editor at Pearson, who pushed us to shape this into a more complete book, and to Jovana San Nicolas-Shirley, our production editor.

Big thanks to Britt Raybould and Aliza Sherman, our technical editors and successful small town entrepreneurs. Also, thanks to our development editor, Ginny Bess Munroe, another small town standout.

Thanks to Liz Strauss for connecting us with each other and with our publisher.

We Want to Hear from You!

As the reader of this book, *you* are our most important critic and commentator. We value your opinion and want to know what we're doing right, what we could do better, what areas you'd like to see us publish in, and any other words of wisdom you're willing to pass our way.

As an editor-in-chief for Que Publishing, I welcome your comments. You can email or write me directly to let me know what you did or didn't like about this book—as well as what we can do to make our books better. *Please note that I cannot help you with technical problems related to the topic of this book. We do have a User Services group, however, where I will forward specific technical questions related to the book.*

When you write, please be sure to include this book's title and author as well as your name, email address, and phone number. I will carefully review your comments and share them with the author and editors who worked on the book.

Email: feedback@quepublishing.com

Mail: Greg Wiegand
         Editor-in-Chief
         Que Publishing
         800 East 96th Street
         Indianapolis, IN 46240 USA

Reader Services

Visit our website and register this book at quepublishing.com/register for convenient access to any updates, downloads, or errata that might be available for this book.

Introduction

Major shifts in the economy, technology, and society have changed the game of business. Business is now forced to play by a different set of rules:

- *When every customer can now talk directly to every other customer, it's like a small town.*

- *When people listen more to what customers say about a company than they listen to the company advertising, it's like a small town.*

- *When it now takes multiple jobs to support a family, it's like a small town.*

- *When the individual human voice is valued over corporate mission statements, it's like a small town.*

- *When everyone online is trying to band together in small communities, it's like a small town.*

- *When everyone wants to buy their products locally, it's like a small town.*

The customers of every company now behave like they live in a small town. As a result, companies now need to play by a new set of rules: small town rules. These new rules apply to small businesses and big brands alike, no matter how big or how urban. Not surprisingly, few people know about these small town rules. However, it is possible to look at what has made small town entrepreneurs successful and apply those rules to every company. For the first time, this book connects the three major shifts that create a small town environment for all business and then teaches the small town rules that help people and companies thrive in this new environment.

Small town doesn't just mean small business or small numbers. Many familiar big brands started in small towns, including Viking Range, L.L. Bean, Sonic Drive-Ins, Longaberger Baskets, Ditch Witch trenching equipment, and Grasshopper lawnmowers. Walmart may be the single most powerful brand to come from a small town and remake the world, affecting both small businesses and huge national brands.

To understand why the small town awareness is especially relevant today, it is important to go back a few years to get perspective on these three major shifts. Remember the economy before 2008? It felt like the stock market always went up, investments always increased in value, and the price of homes always went higher. Back then, there were commercials on TV telling people to mortgage their house, cash out some equity, jump on a hot stock, or join a country club. But, all that has changed.

Economic carnage rocked the financial stability of society with high unemployment rates, tight credit, lower consumer demand, and fewer available resources. At the same time, technology has continued to advance, allowing people to collaborate effectively and instantaneously over great distances and not be tied to a single geographic area. This compounds the effect on society, and shifts people's attention and trust away from multinational corporations toward small and local companies.

Why Look to Small Towns Now?

As a result of these three shifts—society, technology, and the economy—all businesses now face circumstances that feel much like a small town. Small towns have been making parallel shifts over the last century. Innumerable small business people have tried everything they could to survive and thrive within the limits of small towns. The best ones have a reputation for knowing every customer personally and for catering to their customers. That's the public part of successful small-town businesses, but there are many more strategies and tactics behind the scenes: managing multiple lines of income, thinking long term, maintaining frugality, creating community, and building local connections. All seven of these small town rules are included in the seven chapters in this book.

Because small towns are commonly seen as sleepy, slow-moving, and behind the times, few business experts have looked to small town entrepreneurs for lessons. That makes Becky and Barry the exceptions. Barry spoke often in small cities and towns, and he learned that savvy business people exist all over. Becky grew up in a family of small town entrepreneurs, and her work has brought her in contact with hundreds of others. She knows the secrets of small town entrepreneurs inside and out.

Looking closely at small town business and at big city business, this book describes three tectonic shifts: the economy, technology, and society. Each chapter explains one aspect of the change and explains why rural business has relevant insight into that change. The small town rule is explained and adapted to work with any business, and examples are pulled from both rural and urban businesses. The applications for big brands are highlighted, along with some special brand examples. Each chapter concludes with a discussion about whether the change is a permanent shift.

Chapters 1–3: The Change in the Economy

The economic shift was felt like a physical blow. There are big parallels in the national economic transition and the transitions in the rural economy over the last 100 years. Small towns have dealt with limited resources, tight lending, and scarce jobs for a long time. Chapter 1, "Surviving Difficult Economic Times for the Big and Small," deals with surviving difficult economic times by planning for times when income or growth is zero. Rural regions have turned disasters into opportunities, or at least they have learned to prepare for them and take a long-term perspective. Chapter 2, "The New Normal: Profiting When Resources Are Limited," shows that profiting when resources are limited requires spending brainpower before spending dollars. Those limited resources lead to more creative and resilient businesses. Chapter 3, "Adapting to the New Economic Realities of Self-Reliance," teaches businesses and professionals how to adapt to the new economic realities of self-reliance by multiplying lines of income. Brands have to think about brand extension versus brand dilution.

Chapters 4–5: The Change in Technology

The transition in technology also pushes businesses toward small town rules. Chapter 4, "Adapting to the 'Anywhere, Anywhen' Business World," explains geographic advantage and how it disappeared. Working remotely continues to gain ground, even in the largest corporations. The cost of the technology to work anywhere has dropped, until almost any business can use it. Chapter 5, "Forget Advertising: Learn Customer-Driven Communication," deals with community, whether the local community around a small town business or the online community around a major national brand. Online reviews of anything from motels and books to doctors and churches mean that brands can't ignore customer voices.

Chapters 6–7: The Change in Society

The local movement is pushing a transition in society, one that looks a lot like a small town. The renewed interest in healthy neighborhoods, in shopping local, and in small businesses brings every company back to a small town environment. In Chapter 6, "How Big Brands and Small Businesses Are Thinking and Acting Small," small is beautiful. The public trusts small businesses more than large corporations. Economies of scale are called into question by stresses on global supply chains. Some businesses have found ways to successfully stay small while still growing big. Chapter 7, "Going Local, Even When You Are Big," explains why local matters in a global environment. With the new emphasis on all things local, what does it mean to be local as a brand? Small towns are the starting place for shop local campaigns. Every business has a chance to reconnect with its story and where it came from.

With all three of these shifts, the climate for business has been permanently changed. Just like you can never go home again, business can never go back to the way things used to be. Now, every business has to play by small town rules if it wants to thrive and prosper. And this is the only place to learn the rules.

Appendixes: Resource List and Business Ideas Inspired by Small Town Rules

Reading is easy; implementation is not. To help businesses implement the *Small Town Rules*, Appendix A, "Resources for Implementing the Small

Town Rules," includes resources for going more in-depth on each rule. Some resources are specifically for big brands, others for small business. All the resources relate directly to the three major shifts and the seven rules.

Appendix B, "Business Ideas Inspired by the Small Town Rules," includes business ideas that were inspired by the small town rules. The ideas can be used by existing businesses for improvement, innovation, expansion or to change the game.

1

Surviving Difficult Economic Times for the Big and Small

When economic times get tough, the entire country feels more like a small town. The national economy is going through similar changes to what small town economies have gone through in the last 100 years.

Small towns are no stranger to disaster or economic distress. What makes small towns worth looking at is how the people in small towns plan for disasters and how they pull together to get through them. Small towns survive difficult economic times by planning for zero: years when the harvest is zero, months when business income is zero, and times when economic growth is zero. Rural regions turn disasters into opportunities, or have at least learned to prepare for them and take a long-term perspective. The big-brand equivalents of natural disasters can be marketing and PR disasters.

To get perspective on the economic changes that have made the country more like a small town economically, this chapter covers the economic change leading up to and through the Great Recession that started in 2008. It covers how this change has affected major national brands, causing some to slightly falter, some to drop off the Fortune 500, and some to entirely disappear. Stories of small towns facing disaster, pulling together, and planning ahead to endure show how and why small towns survive. Because so many disasters are made worse by the assumptions people make, questioning assumptions becomes more important. Knowing the seasons of business can keep a natural cycle of up and down from being an unforeseen business challenge. Investing long term and saving for those challenging times are small town survival tactics that are applicable to all businesses.

This change in the economy is not going away. The economic hardship of the Great Recession is just the most obvious indicator of a new rule in business: Plan for zero to survive the coming disasters.

The Change: Economic Meltdown

A major part of the news in the past few years has been occupied by the worldwide economic meltdown. The last 10 years have been characterized as the "9/11 Decade." Almost every country has felt the global recession that began in 2008. Although it "officially" ended in June 2009 in the United States, its long-lasting effects are still reflected in high unemployment, lower personal incomes, tight credit markets, and major government-support programs. As the recession ripped through big businesses, industries, and cities, it also destroyed some long-held beliefs about basic market rules and trends.

During much of the 1990s, the American economy enjoyed a long stretch where it seemed there was only one direction the economy could go: up! This included the stock market, everyone's 401(k) retirement accounts, salaries and bonuses, and real-estate prices.

Through 2008, the stock market went on an unprecedented run-up, gaining 65 percent (or more than 4,000 points). It seemed like investing in the stock market was a sure way to make money. Young stockbrokers built their careers on a single strategy: "Buy!" This strategy worked because the market always went up, so there was never a need for any other advice. Mutual funds and stock investments became common in many people's lives. Investment

clubs proliferated. The amount invested in lower-risk Certificates of
Deposit (CD) declined as savings rates also declined and money was
poured into the stock market.

Retirement accounts for the majority of Americans were increasingly tied
to the stock market. Employers shifted away from defined benefit programs toward defined contribution plans. Instead of telling workers how
much they could expect as monthly retirement income, employers began
defining only the amount they would contribute monthly to the workers'
retirement accounts. Those employer contributions went into 401(k) and
403(b) accounts and a myriad of other retirement accounts that mostly held
mutual funds invested in the stock market.

When the market dropped almost 50 percent to 6,500 in 2008, a huge
chunk of many workers' future retirement income was wiped out.
Americans lost $11 trillion of wealth that year alone, which is one quarter
of Americans' net worth.[1] At the time, the press glibly described 401(k)s
being devalued to only "201(k)s." People who were close to retirement had
to keep working. People who were already retired faced living on much
lower incomes or returning to work.

Salaries and bonuses, at least for executives and white-collar workers, were
also on an upward trend through 2008. People came to rely on these annual
increases. Bonuses were expected as a regular and reliable event. In 2009,
the growth in the total cost of compensation for all U.S. businesses was cut
in half. The average cost to employers per hour worked in 2009 rose only
1.5 percent, down from a 3.1 percent increase in 2008.[2]

Home values, the most personal indicator of wealth, rose to unprecedented
levels through 2007. People who owned a home in most of the United
States found that, suddenly, their property was worth much more than
they had originally paid for it. To benefit from that increased value, people
could either sell their homes or simply borrow against them through a
home-equity line. Many homeowners started to use their houses as personal ATMs to borrow against and buy anything they wanted. Perhaps the
slickest home-equity loan pitches were TV commercials from mortgage
companies that offered to cash out some equity so homeowners could join
a country club or jump on the next hot stock.

The entire real-estate market became inflated. Real estate was promoted as
an easy investment, and mortgages were easy to get with no down payment.
"Flipping" houses was a second career for some people. They bought a

property, fixed it up, and turned it around to resell as soon as possible. TV shows sprang up about it, such as *Flip This House*. Ownership of second homes and vacation homes skyrocketed. By the end of 2010, the U.S. saw more than 5.5 million foreclosures, and the number of families affected by foreclosure was estimated at 9 million in 2011.[3]

Commercial real estate also increased in value. At one time, the U.S. had more square feet of retail space per person than any other measured region. At the end of the wave of retail closures, much of that retail space was sitting vacant. Empty big-box stores became a new feature of the urban landscape.

Impact on Brands

Big national brands are not immune to economic, marketing, or public-relations disasters or just plain stupid mistakes. Most big companies do not have the luxury of being "too big to fail" and getting bailed out by the federal government, as many financial institutions (Citibank) and car companies (General Motors and Chrysler) did in 2008.

In fact, no corporation is guaranteed a spot on the Fortune 500 list forever. "There is no law of nature that the most powerful will inevitably remain at the top," writes bestselling business author Jim Collins.[4] Only about 12 percent of the companies have been on the list every year since it started in 1955. Almost 2,000 companies have come and gone.

As a result of the Great Recession of 2008, 71 companies dropped off the Fortune 500 list.[5] The collapse of Bear Sterns and Lehman Brothers were touchstone events. Retailers such as Circuit City, Bombay Co., Goody's, Borders, and Whitehall Jewelers disappeared. Auto brands, such as Saturn and Pontiac, were retired. The venerable Max Factor cosmetics brand was also discontinued. Airlines took a big loss with the closing of Aloha, Champion, ATA, and Skybus.

So, what can cause this kind of fall? Markets can shift, disasters can come at a company from inside or outside, and trend-chasing can damage a company or brand. The small town rules for survival apply just as much in market droughts as in farming droughts. Companies that hold on to frugality and plan for the long term are the ones best positioned for survival.

Shifting Markets and Public-Relations Mistakes

As the book market shifted from print books to eBooks, Borders was slow
to respond. When eBooks and online retail became the largest part of the
book market, Borders was forced into Chapter 11 bankruptcy and eventually liquidated all of its stores. It was unable to overcome competition from
Amazon and Barnes & Noble, which grabbed the eBook market with their
Kindle and Nook electronic readers.

As the movie-rental market shifted from in-store rentals to movies delivered directly to customers' homes and streamed online, Blockbuster never
caught up to Netflix with its mailed DVD movies or with iTunes, which
allows users to download movies. In 2010, Netflix improved its service by
adding unlimited video streaming for a good portion of its movie library.
Consumers were able to watch as many movies as they wanted whenever
they wanted for $8 a month. In response, Blockbuster introduced an unlim-
ited streaming plan, but it was only available to the few customers who
were also current Dish Network subscribers.[6] Blockbuster remains behind
in the rapidly shifting market, because it is unable to keep up.

Having grabbed the lead in the market shift to physical and virtual delivery
of movies, Netflix suffered from bad decisions that created public-relations
problems. In 2011, Netflix damaged its reputation by imposing a major
rate hike, and then split its mail order and streaming services into two different divisions and rebranded the DVD-by-mail service. Facing outraged
customers, Netflix backpedaled on the split into two divisions, but moved
forward with the rate hike.[7]

Marketing strategies can cause other public-relations disasters. Groupon,
in its 2011 Super Bowl ad, made fun of the plight of the Tibetan people.
Although executives apparently thought their online explanation made it
clear that they were actually sensitive to the cause they supported, the ad as
aired looked bad. People reacted to what they saw, and that generated a lot
of negative publicity. Chinese bloggers, in particular, spread the story with
negative commentary. Groupon had been investing heavily in expansion
into China. It had not anticipated that the Chinese would be offended by
the reference to Tibet or that story would spread globally. The ad not only
hurt Groupon's U.S. reputation, it slowed Groupon's attempt to expand
into China.[8]

Major Product Disasters

Events that "stick" to a large corporation can threaten to bring down a company. There are well known examples of Johnson and Johnson's Tylenol (product tampering), Perrier (product contamination) and Honda (brake failures). When British Petroleum's (BP) Deep Horizon oil rig spilled almost 5 million barrels of oil into the Gulf of Mexico in 2010, it became not only the largest accidental oil spill in history, but it also posed a major threat to the company. The direct financial cost has been huge. BP established a claims fund of $20 billion, and $7.5 billion has already been paid out.[9] Oil continues to wash up on the Gulf shores, and may do so for years, as an unknown amount of residual oil remains in the Gulf.[10]

BP managed to survive the spill and initial cleanup, and its long-term outlook was probably what saved the company. Because BP is in the oil-exploration business, it has a built-in long-term view. It takes years, even decades, to discover and develop major energy assets. Development work is intensely regulated (if not very effectively). An individual offshore oil rig can cost millions of dollars, and a single offshore field may contain dozens of rigs. All that long-term investment requires BP to both look far into the future and to maintain a large cash reserve. Both were needed in 2010. BP's $7 billion cash reserve meant it had the money on hand to finance the long and involved shut-down process and begin funding the cleanup trust fund.

Chasing Trends and Shiny Objects, Too!

Many big brands fall victim to chasing trends or getting caught up in "the shiny object syndrome." They want to be involved in any industry that is hot or copy any product or service that is selling exceptionally well. In 2011, these trends included "deal-a-day" services, mobile-location marketing, social-media applications, and anything involving green living. The unquestioned assumption behind chasing business trends is that popular ideas must be profitable. Short-sighted companies tend to jump into situations that don't make sense from the long-term perspective.

Cisco lost money and position chasing a trend when it bought Pure Digital and its wildly successful Flip video camera in March 2009 for $590 million. Two years later, it shut down all its consumer products, including the Flip video camera. CEO John Chambers said that he had to refocus the company after it had disappointed investors and lost credibility.[11]

Barry always tells small business people that if they are looking for the next big trend, it's too late; they've missed it. The same holds true for large companies. Volumes have been written on how to predict trends for big brands, but brand failures happen frequently.

As blogging and social networks became drivers of consumer behavior, major brands have realized that bloggers and online influencers are a good source of promotion. Travel bloggers have been actively courted by tourism destinations. Travel writers for print publications have long received perks and free travel benefits in hopes of attracting positive coverage in magazines and newspaper travel sections. Travel blogger Sheila Scarborough says bloggers are now "the flavor of the month." A few years ago, destinations would ignore online publishers. Now, those same destinations are actively searching for bloggers, chasing the trend of online publishers. In chasing that trend, some only make offers to a few "A list" travel bloggers, who may turn down as many as five offers from destinations per week. Other destinations send offers to almost any travel blogger without sufficient screening. The destinations that do take a long-term approach and carefully screen bloggers can get excellent publicity. The trend-chasing destinations may waste limited funds trying to get the attention of the top travel bloggers or may spend more on poorly screened bloggers and end up with low-quality writing and poor coverage.[12]

In 2011, social-marketing expert Peter Shankman provided an example of the lengths brands will go to to reach select online influencers. As Shankman headed toward his home airport after a long day of travel, he reached out to the local Morton's Steakhouse on Twitter and, as a joke, asked it to meet him at the airport with a steak when he landed. Much to Shankman's surprise, Morton's was there when he arrived, with a to-go meal in hand. The restaurant had navigated approvals, cooking and preparation, traffic and flight schedules to make it work.[13] Why would the brand go to such effort to provide one dinner to one person? Because Shankman is influential. Thousands of people listen to his marketing advice at live events, read his articles on his website, and follow his thoughts on Twitter and Facebook. In past decades, influencers like prominent newspaper columnists might have been the targets of that kind of attention. Today, the trend is chasing online influencers. Morton's certainly got plenty of online attention for the stunt. Other restaurants that try something like it in the future will get less attention, because novelty is short-lived. That compounds the danger for brands chasing trends.

Why Small Towns Survive

Rural entrepreneurs have consistently survived economic hardships and natural disasters for centuries. If they managed to come through the recession any better than urban counterparts or big brands, it's likely because of a fresher memory of the Great Depression. Because rural families are more likely to live close by extended family, it means they grew up spending significant time with Depression-era grandparents who spoke about this difficult time.

For example, the Dust Bowl also started with an economic boom that went bust. Wheat prices soared in the 1910s and 1920s, more than tripling over the course of a decade. At the high point, wheat approached $4 per bushel. With the 1929 market crash, wheat prices dropped 90 percent to 40 cents a bushel. After the price hit this record low, it then declined even more. Then, a second disaster hit: It stopped raining. After two years with drastically reduced or even no income because of the price drop, wheat farmers lost first one crop, then another, as a result of the drought. With no crops to cover the ground, dust began to blow.[14] Becky's grandparents—and many thousands of others—lived through this vicious cycle. Remarkably, two-thirds of the farmers stuck it out and didn't give up. This shaped the rural entrepreneurs' thinking when they grew up hearing these stories.

Disasters are not only a thing of the past. 2011 was a record year for natural disasters in the U.S. An average year sees about 34 major disasters declared by the president. In December 2011, the count was up to 97 federally declared major disasters. FEMA's listing of disaster declarations goes back to 1953, and no single year has had zero disasters.[15]

Today, small towns still pull together to prepare and recover. A survey in Indiana found that rural residents were nearly 12 percent more likely to be prepared for disasters than those who lived in and around urban areas.[16] A modern example of a small town pulling together through adversity is Cherokee, Oklahoma. In August 2006, the town was hit with thunderstorms and destructive downbursts of wind from 80 to 100 miles per hour. Cherokee resident Laura Girty said that the townspeople didn't waste much time in shock over the disaster; they went to work together on repairs and recovery. People found scraps of wood and worked together to cover broken windows. The city crews quickly cleared the streets so that they were passable.

At the airport, the city police chief helped airplane owners salvage what they could from destroyed hangers. His daughter helped by taking pictures for insurance documentation. They all worked together to clear one plane at a time. By the time one out-of-town airplane owner arrived, his plane had been safely removed from his damaged hanger, taken to a more secure area of the airport, and photos had been taken for insurance. The next day, pilots flew undamaged planes to other airports, making room for damaged planes to be moved into the remaining hangers.

Karen Hawkins, owner of the Cherokee Inn and Cherokee Station, had portions of the motel roof and restaurant vent system blown off and scattered for miles. Within hours and over several days, the pieces just started showing back up at her businesses as friendly neighbors recognized the familiar "green roof" and returned them. She claims the returned pieces that she was able to salvage probably saved her $10,000 or more on her repairs.[17]

Although no small town or business could prepare to be completely destroyed, many have been forced to face that kind of reality. One example is Greensburg, Kansas. In May 2007, more than 90 percent of the town's buildings were destroyed by a tornado. There were few fatalities, but almost total destruction of the houses, businesses, and services. The town's 1,500 residents scattered to find places to stay. Most were able to move in with friends or relatives in nearby towns, but some moved away permanently.

Two months after the disaster, several hundred townspeople gathered in Greensburg's Davis Park for a community meal, a speech by rural economic developer Jack Schultz, and leftover fireworks that were rained out on the Fourth of July. Their first enormous task was to design the rebuilding of their town. People gathered around maps, discussed where to rebuild community facilities, how to relocate roads, and how best to rebuild from scratch.

"I've never done a talk like this," Schultz said. "Not for a town so completely destroyed."[18]

Schultz shared the stories of other small towns that were burned down, flooded out, scrubbed by hurricanes, and leveled by tornadoes. He spoke of towns facing devastating economic losses, factory closures, and business failures. He told how those towns came back and managed to make something better. A high-school student asked Schultz how long rebuilding would take. Schultz estimated 5 to 10 years.

Ruth Ann and Bob Wedel lost almost every single thing in their bulk foods business in Greensburg. It was supposed to be their retirement business. The two of them successfully built it from scratch, expanding to six employees. It looked like they would be able to sell the company at a profit as they approached retirement. Instead, after the tornado, they dug through the rubble of their store, salvaging only a few items.

To survive, they merged with a friend's catering business. By the two-month mark, the Wedels were serving lunches every day under tents in a parking lot. They were hoping to move up from tents to a car port the next day.

Ruth Ann explained some of the difficulties of locating a temporary trailer to work from, finding a site for it, and rebuilding their original building downtown. Ultimately, the Wedels decided not to reopen the store. Ruth Ann took a position with the Greensburg GreenTown organization, working on rebuilding the town in a green way.[19]

The town government's website proudly proclaims, "Greensburg: Stronger, Better, Greener!" Dozens of national companies have been involved in the ecologically sound rebuilding. A chain of eco-homes is being constructed, and businesses and services are back up and running. The entire town is being rebuilt from scratch.

Small towns are no strangers to disaster or economic distress. What makes small towns worth emulating is how the people plan for those disasters and how they pull together to get through them.

The Small Town Rule: Plan for Zero

Farmers plan for years when the harvest is zero because of drought or another natural disaster. Businesses plan for months when income may be zero following economic hard times or a business disaster, like a fire or flood. Small towns plan for times when growth is zero because of the loss of a key employer or natural disaster. Planning for zero is the small town answer to knowing that disaster is possible. There are three ways to get ready for those zero times: question assumptions, know the seasons and cycles, and invest for the long term.

Question Assumptions

Few disasters are completely unpredictable, whether natural or manmade. What stops people from preparing for or preventing disaster is the set of assumptions that underlie a "business as usual" mindset. To survive economic turmoil and natural disasters, rural entrepreneurs have learned to question assumptions that may be common in other businesses.

In the book *The Worst Hard Time*, author Timothy Egan shares some of the commonly accepted beliefs that existed at the time of the Dust Bowl. Some of these commonly held beliefs turned out to be incredibly destructive to the rural economy:[20]

- **"Rain follows the plow."** Plowing the surface was said to release moisture and cause rain. That's only half right; it does release soil moisture, but it doesn't make it rain. Translating this idea to business means questioning whether the cause and effect are really there. Many small businesses think that sales naturally follow marketing, but if prospects are not followed up and cared for, they will never turn into customers. Hard work building trusted relationships is what produces sales.

- **"The soil is the one resource that can never be exhausted."** This was printed in farming instruction manuals of the day. Of course, soil, like any other natural resource or natural system, has limits. Planting the same crops year after year without adding any inputs will deplete all the available nutrients in the soil. Leaving the soil tilled or disturbed for long periods leaves it vulnerable to wind and water erosion. In business, are there any resources that are really "inexhaustible?" What would happen if they were gone? Some businesses act as though there is an inexhaustible supply of customers, as they burn and churn through buyers, never servicing the ones they already have. Unfortunately, many businesses treat vendors and employees in the same fashion.

- **"Anybody can make money in this boom."** In the boom time of the 1920s, suitcase farmers began showing up to plant the ground, then leaving until time to harvest the crop and hopefully rake in the profits. When the price crashed, they disappeared, leaving the ground plowed up and exposed. The idea of easy money in the boom is common in business. Speculators rush in to the latest fad for quick profits. People dive into subjects that they know nearly nothing about in the hopes of making a big score. Entire businesses are built on the idea that the rising tide will lift all boats. Of course, the tide will turn eventually. The boom is always followed by a bust. The speculators rush out for the next big thing, and many businesses are lost. It comes back down to the fundamentals. Only superior execution and experience result in profit.

- **"New technology makes things better."** Tractors changed the farming game in the 1920s, making it possible for one person to work 10 times as much ground. This actually magnified everything: profits in the boom and devastation in the bust. In the world of modern business, technology is still magnifying profits in boom time and the potential for losses in the bust. It seems almost heresy to question the use of technology, but it's necessary. One obvious example is the computerized trading programs that now control a large share of stock trades. These can make enormous profits for some and can reduce other companies' market values all the way to zero in microseconds. Just because something is technologically possible doesn't make it good business.

Even today, entrepreneurs can be so focused on the status quo that it is incredibly difficult to change the pattern. Becky watched as one farmer faced this challenge in 1992 at an agricultural workshop. An expert advised him to skip fertilizing his hay field to achieve what he wanted. The farmer said, incredulously, "But what would I do if I didn't fertilize?" He couldn't see past the way he had always done things. The idea of changing was completely foreign. Entrepreneurs of all sizes and big brands face the same challenge: seeing past the way things have always been done and making changes.

Know the Seasons and Cycles

Small town entrepreneurs largely missed out on the economic boom. People in most rural areas saw little change in salaries and home values.

While the stock market was rising, many people in rural areas didn't have the extra money for luxuries like stock-market investments. This gives rural people perspective that has been lost in the larger economy, one that is more closely tied to the baseline value of things. In a world gone crazy with boom and bust cycles of inflated values followed by deep crashes, the small town view of natural cycles and seasons has become more realistic.

Business people work alongside farmers and ranchers in small towns. Being closer to farming is a good thing in this case, because farmers were some of this country's first entrepreneurs. Farmers have three secrets to share with successful businesses and brands: They work with the seasons, they aren't afraid to invest when needed, and they take a long-term view.

Farmers must pay attention to seasons: There's a time to plant, a time to reap, and a time to prepare. Businesses have to pay attention to seasons, too, because they come into play in business. There's a time to plant new projects, a time to reap new rewards, and a time to prepare for what's next.

Farming seasons are the same now as they have been for millennia. Planting must be done at the right time or there will be no crop. It can't be delayed or put off. The farmer can't cram it in later. Every business or brand has to spend time planting seeds for the future through marketing, training, and research and development. These can't be successfully delayed any more than farmers can hold off on planting crops.

After the planting is done, it's time for the growing season. It's inevitable that problems will happen during this season. Weeds will grow, competing with the crop for nutrients and sunlight. Rains may come at the wrong time or fail completely. Insects and disease may destroy some, or even all, of the crop. The farmer has to work to keep the crop healthy, while fending off treatable problems, like pests, but nothing can be done about the weather. Every business or brand has a growing season, as projects and investments are maturing. During that time, businesses will experience problems, just like farmers experience weeds. Needed resources may elude businesses, much like rain eludes farmers in a drought. That means businesses have to invest time defending their projects from problems, like farmers defend their crops.

Harvest is a critical time. A week of delay because of weather can erase an entire year's profit. Usually, though, harvest is a time of happy hard work, as the year's profit is reaped. Harvest isn't just for farmers. It's also for business. "That's our harvest." It's a common phrase among small town businesses to explain their busiest or most profitable time of the year. Big brands have harvest times, too, as their promotions and projects reap sales.

Then, the slow time comes. Fields are left fallow, usually during winter, waiting for the next planting time. Farmers spend winter busy repairing equipment, making decisions on the future production and planning ahead. For businesses and brands, big payoffs are frequently followed by dead times. Every brand and business must dedicate some time to the type of planning and decision-making that farmers do during winter. That planning must be done before the cycle can begin again, and new projects can be launched.

Rural businesses and entrepreneurs often adapt their businesses to the local farming schedule. Schools, sports, businesses, and entire towns may close down during harvest. A recent rural Australian headline announced the local sports team had been forced to forfeit a game on account of harvest. This closeness has kept rural entrepreneurs in touch with the natural cycles of farming and business. All businesses experience cycles, even though they aren't farming.

Retail's busiest time is the holiday season. Retail businesses may make one-third to one-half of their total annual sales in just two months: November and December. Accountants are crazy with work in April. For real-estate professionals, sales peak in the spring and summer. Manufacturers may adapt to the availability of materials depending on the season. Service businesses are dependent on the ebb and flow of their customers' underlying businesses.

Companies that are out of touch with cycles may find their efforts perpetually wasted, like the retailer who cuts back on inventory before the holidays to save money. Being aware of these cycles makes it easier to recognize them. "Oh, this is one of those winters. Wonder what I can do to get ready for the next planting season?"

Even in the online world, there are business cycles. Online retail isn't immune from holiday rushes. In fact, online retailing takes center stage on "Cyber Monday," as employees shop for bargains on their return to work after Thanksgiving. It started in the U.S., but it's now a global online-shopping event.

Startup businesses also have cycles. Entrepreneurs work to plant the seeds of a new startup, guard the growing business against intruding problems, and hope to harvest a big profit through a stock offering or a buyout. Today, all entrepreneurs need to be prepared to go through all stages of business. Be prepared for "an overnight success" to be at least a 5- to 10-year journey. The prize now goes to those who compete long enough, survive, and build something that has value. Congratulate the company owners that have been in business for 10 or 20 years.

Invest Long Term

The view of farmers as uneducated individuals in overalls is long outdated. Farmers were quick to adopt smartphones and, before that, two-way and CB radios. Long-distance communication was necessary, not a luxury. Today, farmers must buy several kinds of expensive equipment. They invest a quarter of a million dollars in a piece of equipment, like a combine (grain harvester), fully knowing that they are only going to use it for one week out of the year. With advances in farming technology, the average family farm doubles in size every generation. The technology that makes that possible also requires a big investment in training. What good is that new GPS-guided cultivation system if no one knows how to use it? Today's family farm has more assets under management than any non-farmer would believe, usually well into the millions of dollars in land, equipment, livestock, and other assets. Because half-million dollar tractors are common, farmers, like any other business owners, carefully weigh each major equipment purchase. It takes long-term financial planning to amortize the cost of a half-million dollar purchase over 10 or more years of production.

Many dairy farms have enviably detailed business plans with financial projections that would make any MBA proud. The razor-thin margins of dairy farming mean that long-term planning is necessary. While most people are familiar with the stereotype of farmers as hard-nosed and practical, they would be surprised at the practical business planning and long-term perspective that now goes into farming. It is a professional entrepreneurial endeavor.

The supporting principle (and a seemingly contradictory one) is to get by without investing anything at all. Farmers excel at this; it's how they can afford to pay half a million dollars for a massive tractor. Part of planning ahead is that they never throw away anything they might be able to use later. Most farms have a corner filled with old equipment. On Becky's farm, the collection of useful junk includes a horse-drawn wagon and an early combine, a grain drill with steel wheels, an old feed grinder, and innumerable pieces of scrap metal. Every so often, a mechanical part or a piece of metal from one of them will be just the thing to make a repair on a newer piece of equipment. When they installed a new solar panel and water pump to provide water for cattle, the iron for the frame to mount the panel came out of the scrap heap. That's the small town rule: Adopt the latest technology, but don't throw away anything that you can still use. There is a reason for the phrase "farmer engineering." A good farmer can fix almost anything with duct tape and baling wire.

Wheat farmers in northwest Oklahoma also take a long-term approach. Their crop doesn't succeed every year. One year may be hailed out, too dry, too wet, too hot, or any number of things that cause the crop to fail. As a result, one year out of five is a loss. One year out of five is a bumper crop (more than expected). The other three years fall somewhere in between. They may even have two crop losses in a row, so that's two years with no income. This means they must have a long-term perspective. It's not enough to save money for lean years; they must also plan ahead for failure and for success. When Becky looks out her back window at home, she sees the wheat field farmed by her neighbors, the Percivals. Over the last several years, their wheat crop has required the Percivals to plan long term. The first year was average, with average yields and price. The second year was very good, with a decent price, and really good yields. The third year, the price was up, way up, but it didn't matter. The entire crop was lost to rain, and it rotted in the field. They plowed every bit of it under. The fourth year, the price was not too bad, and yields were about average. The fifth year, it started raining at the beginning of harvest. It looked like it might be another total loss, but they got in the fields late, and they managed to save enough to get about a quarter of their usual income. The sixth year was a drought. The yields were very poor, but quality was terrific and the price was good. Their income was about half of an average year. So, that's one great year, two average years, one zero, one year that was a quarter, and one year at half the usual income. Surviving that kind of wild swing takes significant long-term planning. The Percivals built their long-term plan by diversifying their income base through a second crop: cattle.

Becky also uses long-term planning in her farming. Back in 1992, she attended a workshop on forage management. One piece of advice stuck with her: "Stockpiled native forage can save you during a drought." She and her husband remembered that advice and changed their grazing practices.

It took a long time to come up, but in 2011, an exceptional drought hit Texas, Oklahoma, New Mexico, and Kansas. Because they had made the long-term decision to hold 160 acres of native grass in reserve, they had a place to move their cattle long after their regular pastures were devastated by the heat and drought. It was tough to hold that land aside in the good years, but that long-term perspective paid off in saving their cattle during the bad year.

Although most businesses don't need a quarter-of-a-million dollar harvester to use for one week each year, every entrepreneur has to make decisions about investing in equipment, people, and expenses. These are long-term planning questions. Smart businesses and brands follow the lead of the dairy farmers with their detailed business plans and run the numbers. Simple useful-life calculations can clarify big purchases.

How long should a business limp along with free software or online services that "kinda work" before subscribing to a paid service that does exactly what is needed? Is a $600 copy of Adobe PhotoShop required, or will the free Aviary image-editing service work? Run the numbers. An entrepreneur who needs to do one quick photo edit per month can't justify the $600 purchase as quickly as a professional photographer who edits photos for 6 hours a day.

Long term has a different meaning online. In the 6 years of the wheat crop previously mentioned, the online world has been transformed yet again. Six years ago, YouTube and Twitter didn't exist yet. So, a long-term perspective in the online world might be as short as a year. That doesn't relieve online businesses from looking long term. Especially as new models evolve quickly online, there will be periods of no income for the entrepreneur.

It can seem like a big stretch for any small business owner to think of 1 or even 2 full years with zero income. That's the lesson from the farmers. Small town businesses may not be sitting on a 2-year cash cushion, but they at least have the awareness of the risks.

Applying Small Town Rules to Big Brands Survival: Planning for Zero

Planning for zero doesn't come easy in the corporate environment. The idea of working by the seasons and natural cycles is far removed from the glass towers and lush campuses of corporate headquarters. But, natural cycles still rule, and planning for zero still means questioning assumptions, knowing the seasons, and investing for the long term.

One company that truly gets investing for the long term is Vanguard Investments. Its strategy is to stay the course. Vanguard clients hear that phrase over and over: Stay the course. Vanguard says the basis for its success is simple: "choose the right asset mix, invest at cost, focus on the long term and stick with the plan." It stresses that it does not get caught up in the market swings or get emotional in its investment strategy. As a result, 75 percent of its funds have outperformed the market.[21]

Planning Ahead Is a Survival Strategy

Southwest, the only U.S. airline to make money consistently over the last 25 years, is always prepared. It bought oil futures when it felt that fuel prices would skyrocket. This allowed the company to lock in that major cost and remain profitable. Southwest also does not spend all the earnings it makes. It always retains earnings for the future. It's possible that its Texas roots, while not exactly small town, gives it a closer tie to the rural realities of natural cycles.

Summary: Things Don't Always Go Up

The economic change that started in 2008 continues to affect business worldwide. The economy cannot be counted on to always go up. Natural and man-made disasters have hit brands and businesses. The economic climate for all business seems much more like a small town.

The Small Town Rule: Plan for Zero

The corollaries:

1. **Question assumptions.** Believing the prevailing view can be deadly. No matter how stable the current situation seems to be, change can happen. This could be the hardest rule to follow, because every business person is too close to his own assumptions to see what they are.

2. **Know there are seasons and cycles, and plan ahead.**
   Know the planting times and the harvesting times. Expect
   there to be a winter dead time in every type of business.

3. **Invest long term in the future.** Those zero years are coming, even when everything seems to be going well. Hold
   some stockpiles in reserve. During those up years, set aside
   some for the future and use some profits to make smart
   investments in the business.

A Look Ahead

Will businesses always need to plan for zero? Yes. The cycles of business will never stop. The turning of the seasons will never change, no
matter how far removed from farming a business may be. The economy and disasters will both always be factors in business.

The economy is going to remain unpredictable. It is globally connected, and a problem in one location can ripple across the world.
The complexity of today's stock markets adds another level of uncertainty. Computerized trading, dark pools of trading outside the established markets, and high-frequency trading all compound market
swings and volatility. All the more reason for smart brands and entrepreneurs to plan for zero.

Disasters will always happen. That means smart businesses and
brands will expect disasters and plan ahead.

Powerhouse Small Town Brands

Winnebago Industries

Forest City, Iowa: Population 4,100

When consumers think about recreational vehicles (RVs), one brand name pops to the top: Winnebago. It began as a typical 1950s small town economic development story that took an unusual turn.

In 1958, Forest City, Iowa, was dealing with an economic downturn. Several local businessmen convinced a California company to open a travel-trailer factory in Forest City to boost its economy. The manufacturing got off to a rough start, but the local community turned the story around. Five locals bought the operation from the California group. One of the men who helped recruit the business, John K. Hanson, stepped in as president.

To improve the quality of its trailers, Winnebago started making almost all its own furniture and components. It also introduced the "Thermo-Panel" wall system, which was lightweight, strong, and insulating.

Winnebago Industries still makes almost all component parts from scratch, promoting its "heartland of the U.S.A." location as a contributor to its quality. It also keeps the manufacturing dies and molds, so replacement parts can be recreated even years after production stops.

To produce all these parts itself, Winnebago created more than ten major divisions within the company. These divisions extrude aluminum into ladders and frames, stitch soft goods like bedspreads, do rotational molding of tanks and wheel wells, build cabinets, stamp metal, prepare the chassis, and mold fiberglass.

Revenues topped $1 billion in 2004, and more than 400,000 units have been produced during the company's 50-year history. It produces RVs under four different brand names and manufactures parts for other companies and commercial vehicles.

The headquarters are still in Forest City, with additional production facilities in Charles City, Iowa, and Middlebury, Indiana. The company employs
approximately 2,000 people.

Winnebago Industries has followed the small town rule of looking long-
term by choosing to invest in manufacturing all its own components and
maintaining replacement part availability for years after production. It also
followed the small town rule of diversifying its revenue streams by marketing under four brands and by manufacturing parts for other companies.

2

The New Normal: Profiting When Resources Are Limited

When resources are limited, it's just like a small town. The entire business world is in the middle of a situation that feels a lot like what small towns have faced for years. Lending all over the country has tightened up, much like the small town lending situation. Lower consumer demand makes the national market parallel the typical small town market. Limits on the availability of a skilled workforce bring national brands and businesses squarely into small town territory.

The survival skills of small town entrepreneurs are now relevant to all businesses. Frugality calls for creative thinking in business. Small town businesses have long been creative in the face of limited resources, and now all businesses need to be. Small town businesses that have always been frugal have survived and can offer lessons for big businesses. They have dealt with limited credit availability, lower consumer demand, and shortages of skilled workers. Rather than spending money to solve resource limitations, small town businesses first spend their brainpower. They get creative about finding alternative financing and a workforce.

This is a long-term change for the business industry. Limited resources are part of a new reality that calls for a new rule: Spend creativity before spending dollars.

The Change: Resources Are Now Limited

Economic changes have forced a new reality of limited resources for all entrepreneurs. Traditionally, this was a challenge only in the early stages of a business, but it has now crept into every stage. This consistently takes the form of limited commercial bank credit, lower consumer demand, and fewer skilled workers.

Although interest rates are at a record low, loans and mortgages are no longer sure things. Lending standards have been tightening from 2008 into 2012. For people who lost jobs or part of their income, it has become even harder to qualify for any type of loan. Home mortgages have been the subject of fraud and loose paperwork-processing practices. The high number of foreclosures contributed to the recession, and now, much tighter standards are being applied. At one time, home buyers could qualify to borrow 100 percent of the cost of a new home (or even more); but now, restrictions are being placed on the amount of mortgages. This is not just true in the U.S.; Canada has tightened lending practices, and the United Kingdom has restricted several types of high-risk loans in a 2009 Banking Act.[1]

Lower consumer demand has also struck businesses in the bottom line. After a huge contraction in demand in 2008, an even further contraction happened in 2010.[2] There seems to be consensus that the Great Recession has changed consumer-spending habits for the foreseeable future. With fewer jobs, a lower stock market, and restricted credit, consumers don't feel like they have enough spending money to increase their buying.

Another limited resource is the workforce. Even with surprisingly high unemployment, many industries face a shortage of skilled workers. A high-school diploma is no longer enough education to achieve middle-class wages. Expensive post-secondary education or four-year degrees are increasingly required for basic prosperity. At the same time, more students are dropping out prior to graduating high school. (The rate can be as high as one-third of all high-school students.) Nursing and many other skilled healthcare jobs face critical and ongoing worker shortages. Trained engineers in many specialties are also in drastically short supply.

Even jobs calling for relatively little training still face a workforce shortage, because they require "soft skills," such as reliability, team work, communication, and punctuality. Lack of these types of skills pushes many workers from job to job. As a result, even lower-skilled industries and positions face shortages of quality workers. Increasingly, businesses find themselves looking at a large pool of applicants, with no quality candidate to hire.

Impacts on Big Brands: Low Consumer Demand Hits Where It Hurts Everyone

Brands that built their dominance on wooing the U.S. middle class have run into a problem: The middle class isn't buying as much. Brands find their sales squeezed and are forced to reposition themselves up to the high-end or down for bargain shoppers. Procter & Gamble (P&G) and H.J. Heinz adjusted their consumer product mix to reduce their focus on the middle-class shopper. Many middle-class shoppers are now buying more budget-priced staples, so the companies are responding with more bargain-priced items. P&G previously made best-in-class products at premium prices that targeted the middle class. Now, it focuses on the two ends of the buyer spectrum, top and bottom, rather than the middle class. Citigroup analysts have created an index of brands that are well positioned to capitalize on this trend, which it calls the "Consumer Hourglass Theory."[3]

Lower consumer demand and uncertainty has forced major brands to take a more defensive financial position, retaining cash and reducing investments in human resources. The companies that are doing well are retaining more cash on their balance sheet. In 2010, U.S. corporations among Standard & Poor's (S&P) 500-stock index were sitting on a record $2.6 trillion of cash.[4] Although this may not seem like a bad thing at first glance, it comes at a cost of not making new investments, such as hiring additional full-time employees. Instead, they hire part-time workers or outsource the work to the contingent work professionals. This ultimately keeps the unemployment rate high and consumer demand low, which circles back to the big brands. It becomes difficult to break this cycle.

To further shore up their defensive financial position, big brands that can qualify for credit have increased their borrowing. They know it may be more difficult to arrange financing in an uncertain future. The companies in the S&P 500 have borrowed more than $300 billion in extra cash. Cheap borrowing rates make this attractive for companies that want extra flexibility and financial stability.[5]

Why Small Towns? Because Resources Have Always Been Tight for Rural Business

Small town business people conserve because being frugal has always been a way of life. Frugality is a standard joke among small town people. Some will tell you that their grandmother still has a drawer full of bread wrappers. There's an entire generation of rural people who survived the Great Depression in the 1930s, and they don't throw away anything they might need.

That principle of frugality works well in small town business, too. When Becky's mother, Glenna Mae Hendricks, needed shelves for wine in the stock room at her small town liquor store, she didn't order expensive industrial shelving or new wine-storage racks. She took old bookshelves and filled them with cardboard wine boxes with dividers for bottles. She already had the shelves, and the boxes came with each order of new stock. That made workable storage racks in the tradition of frugal "farmer engineering" at no extra expense to her business. Twenty years later, those frugal wine shelves are still there, and they still work.

The generation that survived the stock market and banking collapse of the Depression didn't tend to invest in stocks. Most of them kept significant amounts of money in low-risk Certificates of Deposit (CD). Because they invested in CDs, they missed the huge run-up in stock values, but they also missed out on the cutting losses of the 2008 Great Recession.

Although they aren't necessarily investing in CDs, smart small town business people also build cash reserves. Even though they have to be frugal to save up those reserves, they make it a priority because it builds flexibility for their small business over many things that can't be controlled. They can respond to market changes, weather financial storms, and move quickly when needed because they have extra reserves to tap.

Many people remember the heady days during the Internet bubble of 1999, when an entrepreneur could write a business plan and an angel or venture capital investor would give him $1 million to launch it (or at least the press made it seem that way). More than a decade later, entrepreneurs now brag about how *little* money it took to launch their business. In the Great

Recession, when it comes to starting a company, frugality is more likely to be a hallmark of success. In 2006, a Wells Fargo poll found that the average small business owner started her company with $10,000. Seventy-three percent surveyed funded their businesses with their own savings.[6] Actually, having too much money in a business launch can be wasteful. It can lead to lazy and unwise decisions. Eric Ries studied the science of successful startups, building on his own experience. In his book, *The Lean Startup*, he says "...it isn't about being cheap [but is about] being less wasteful and still doing things that are big."[7]

Loans and mortgage lending have always been tight in small towns because conservative lending is the rule in this environment. Local bankers scrutinize every proposal and every business plan that is used to apply for a loan. Small town bankers typically personally inspect businesses, actually visiting the premises before approving loans. Although a business owner might get away with overstating the value of a business to a big-city banker who will never visit, it is much harder to get away with doing so when the small town bank sends two loan officers to personally appraise the value of the building or inventory. The banker also knows most borrowers' families, sometimes going back for generations.

When small town banks abandon those traditional conservative practices, it can result in their collapse. *Time* magazine reported the "Death of a Small Town Bank" about Community Bank & Trust in Cornelia, Georgia. Like many other small town banks, it used to send loan officers to personally inspect all property used as collateral, the bankers relied on personal knowledge of borrowers, and the careful nature of small town bankers directed the investments they chose. During a real-estate boom in 2006, the bank moved away from that style of small town banking. Out-of-town people bought vacation homes in the area, which started price increases. As the values shot up, looser lending standards were adopted. Soon, it was easier for any borrower to get a loan from Community Bank & Trust for real-estate development. That direct community connection between borrower and lender was stretched out as more and more questionable loans were approved to take advantage of the boom. But, the boom did not last forever. Property values slid, investments were lost, and increasing numbers of the landowners were unable to repay bank loans. The entire financial position of the bank was compromised. In 2010, it was closed by the FDIC, and it was a blow to the small town perception of community.[8]

Lower Consumer Demand

Small town businesses have long had to survive with lower customer demand because of three factors: a smaller customer base, lower per-capita incomes, and competition from larger retail markets.

Small town businesses have always had smaller customer bases than their urban counterparts. It's a simple matter of available population: Fewer people geographically means fewer potential customers. Small town businesses that survive have to adapt to this reality. Although an ultra-niche specialty shop can survive in a metropolitan area, it could not survive in a rural area. In big cities, specialty wine shops can carry only 100 selected wines because they have more potential customers from which to draw buyers. In a small town, stores have to make up for the smaller customer base by carrying a broader line of merchandise.

Although national businesses were built on high consumer spending, rural businesses were capped by lower per-capita incomes in their narrow customer base. In most rural areas, per-capita incomes increased more slowly than the national average. Once again, small-town businesses have long had to deal with a reality that is just now hitting national businesses.

Competition from larger markets (and the Internet) also narrows some of the potential customer demand in small towns. Their customers are driving great distances to "shop in the big city" for fun. During the holiday season, locals pack up for a full day of shopping in bigger cities, where they can do all of their shopping at one time with more stores. The feeling is that it's fun to be in a place with more shops, more activity, and more people. The local appliance-store owner hates to hear that anyone drove to the nearby big city and bought a new refrigerator from the big-box retailer. That means he missed out on the profit of the initial sale, and he hasn't yet realized that this creates a huge opportunity in service rather than relying on sales.

The concept of "retail capture" shows just how much demand small towns lose. The Oklahoma State University Cooperative Extension Service uses these statistics to explain how small towns capture only a limited amount of the average retail trade. When all the retail sales in a small town are totaled and divided per person, it never equals what the average person spends on retail. Residents have made only part of their retail purchases in town. Where are those other retail dollars going? They are spent online and in cities. For towns under 5,000 in population, the retail sales captured averages only 80 to 90 percent of the average purchases per person. It's even worse in towns with a population under 1,000. Those small towns capture, on average, only 50 to 60 percent of the retail purchases their residents make. Big towns collect those other sales, and their retail sales figures may capture 100 to 140 percent of the average purchases of their own residents.[9] Small town businesses have learned to survive with limited consumer demand that is now affecting all big brands and urban small businesses.

A Shortage of Skilled Workforce

Generally speaking, because of a lack of higher education, most rural areas start at a disadvantage when it comes to finding skilled workers. All the qualified workers are already employed, leading to low unemployment rates. In some rural counties, unemployment rates were below 3 percent, while the national rate remained over 8.5 percent in the U.S. For example, rural Roger Mills County, Oklahoma, had an unemployment rate of 2.4 percent when the national rate was 8.6 percent in September 2011. Low unemployment rates indicate that the pool of available workers is very shallow. Many unemployed people who could have been available to be hired have disqualified themselves with a DUI or drug conviction, an incomplete education, or a just plain "scary" work history. The workforce is also getting older, along with the aging population. That's the typical small town workforce: They are either already employed, under-qualified, disqualified, or aging out. Many promising young people in high school leave town just as soon as they possibly can after graduating. The result: Rural entrepreneurs learned to be creative in how they find and use labor.

The Small Town Rule: Spend Creative Brainpower Before You Spend Dollars

Being creative is a small town's answer to limited resources. The corollaries are to conserve and make being frugal a way of life, to be creative in financing and workforce.

Creative Financing

Because traditional bank lending is so tight in small towns, many small town entrepreneurs learn to bootstrap instead of asking banks for financing. When they want to expand, they look for innovative ways to get the money. Some save up for months—or even years—to purchase new equipment without a loan. They sell off excess inventory or older equipment to finance purchases.

Still others look to non-traditional lenders, like rural utility relending funds. Rural utility relending funds come from USDA grants to rural utility cooperatives. The cooperatives can use the money to create a revolving loan fund for small businesses. One participating cooperative is Northwestern Electric Cooperative in Woodward, Oklahoma. They make low-interest loans to area small businesses so those businesses can purchase equipment.

Because these non-traditional programs vary based on location, they can be difficult to find. Kansas has created a map showing its local business capital-funds programs. It included angel-investor funds, matching-loan programs, regional foundations, USDA lending programs, and rural cooperatives that give loans. Each county has a customized list of the programs available to businesses. Unfortunately, few states offer such a clear guide to capital-funds programs. Entrepreneurs in other states must perform more of the research themselves.

No matter the problem, small-business people everywhere have the option to creatively finance their business. Throwing money at the problem, buying a way out, is not always going to work. Even entrepreneurs with large venture funding or significant lines of credit could benefit from taking a creative rather than "spendy" approach to problems.

Creative financing methods include the following:

- **Factoring.** This method allows businesses to sell accounts receivable to a third party (such as The Receivables Exchange) for immediate cash. Factoring is expensive because it can cost up to 15 percent of the receivable. This may work for a growing company, but it is not a method of financing for a company that is shrinking or losing money.

- **Retirement accounts.** Borrowing money from an IRA or 401(k) can be tempting, as many workers may have significant amounts in them. For quick financing, entrepreneurs can take a 60-day interest-free loan from these retirement accounts. There are no penalties if it is paid back in this time frame.

- **Government grants.** These programs require research at local, state, and federal levels. The granting agencies include the

USDA, the Department of Commerce, and the Treasury Department. They come with names like SBIR, STTR, and SBIC. Typically, they are specific and technical in nature and come with reporting strings attached.

- **Peer-to-peer lending (P2P).** It is now possible for business owners to go online and get funding from people they do not know at websites such as Prosper.com and Lending Club. The amount paid for the loan depends on the business owner's credit score, the economy, the length of the loan, and whether the business has a compelling story.

- **Crowdfunding.** This is a sister method to P2P. Small businesses can now get people to contribute to their financing in exchange for something (other than money). This is a different source of funding because the money is not repaid. The rewards for donors range from receiving the first products to having a product named after them. Popular sites that facilitate crowdfunding include IndieGoGo and Kickstarter. Success with crowdfunding depends on both the emotional appeal of the business idea and the strength of the business person's network.

- **Microfinancing.** Although this is relatively new in the United States, these small loans up to $10,000 are gaining popularity. Loans are based on the entrepreneur's experience, passion, market opportunity, and sales. Organizations include Accion USA, Grameen Bank, and Kiva.

- **Supplier or wholesaler financing.** This method works with the business's supply chain to get the money that it needs. It usually works best with a smaller, local supplier who really wants the business and is willing to work flexibly. Tony Hsieh, CEO of Zappos, said this type of financing was critical to the company's growth.

- **Business plan competitions or other contests.** When all else fails, try to win the money! Many regional and national competitions give away substantial amounts of money, such as the MIT $100K Entrepreneurship Challenge, The GE Ecomagination Challenge, and the Amazon Web Services Start Up Challenge.

- **Business incubators.** Some new small businesses can get seed money, mentorship, and other similar services to get started in a business incubator. These types of organizations have a great track record of success, which include Excelerate Labs and TechStars. Local versions also exist in many areas.

- **Barter.** Swap products or services, not money. Before there was currency, there was only bartering (trading). The U.S. Department of Commerce estimates that 25 percent of the world's trade is still done this way. Barter can save money, move unused inventory, and find new customers. Bartering can be done directly with another business or through a barter exchange, like IMS Barter.

- **Form a cooperative.** Cooperative businesses operate like any other business, but with different decision-making and profit-distribution procedures. The key feature of a cooperative is group ownership. This makes it appropriate for community-owned or worker-owned businesses. A few states, including Minnesota, now allow hybrid cooperatives that include features of limited liability companies. Hybrids can allow outside investment capital.

- **Direct public offerings.** Direct public offerings are smaller stock issues than the traditional initial public offering (IPO). They also cost the issuing business less. Shares can be sold to customers, employees, suppliers, and supporters. Offerings of $50,000 up to $3 million are typical.

- **Royalty financing.** For businesses with established sales, royalty financing makes sense. The amount of payments is tied to sales, ensuring that lean months won't break the business. Rather than a bank, this type of financing is likely to come from an investor or economic development agency.[10]

These 13 alternative financing tools give businesses the options to achieve their business goals without relying solely on bank financing. When any one resource is limited, smart small businesses take a creative look at ways to get around that limit.

Being Frugal

Being cheap is good for your business. One of Barry's favorite expressions is that, in business, "Too much money can make you stupid." (And he follows it with, "I know, you hope you become a blithering idiot!") It has been shown that more companies are financially successful in the long run with fewer startup resources than if they spent lavishly.

According to Mike Maples, companies having an abundance of capital led some startups to "pursue losing strategies for too long at the detriment of the winning strategies." He said that some of the most successful start-ups were hyper-frugal, including Cisco, Google, Yahoo!, and Microsoft. Maples said that there is an inverse correlation between money required by a startup and its potential chaotic success, so in some ways, the current economic difficulties may be leading to the successful companies of the future.[11]

A survey by *Forbes Insights* found small businesses in Canada said that eco-nomic adversity had actually improved their business.

Canadian SMEs in the survey said the recession essentially forced them to become better businesses. Overall, 64% said they are planning more effec-tively, and an identical 64% agreed they are smarter today about running their businesses than they were before the recession. 68% said they feel they are in a stronger position today than they were prior to the downturn.[12]

Reducing Startup Costs

Starting a business does not need to cost a lot of cash. Entrepreneurs must be frugal with their money, especially in the startup phase, before sales are regular. Here are some simple guidelines:

- **Spend less designing logos and websites.** Consider using crowd-sourced design services, such as the Chicago-based crowdSPRING. On these sites, designers compete for projects, and that can result in lower prices. Barry never spent more than $500 on a logo or $1,000 on a website to start. As the business' needs evolve, more money will need to be spent later.

- **Use free or inexpensive software for office needs.** Try Wordpress for websites, Highrise for a customer-relationship management system, and Google Docs for office software; these are excellent starter choices.

- **Work virtually and hire freelancers to do the work.** Always strive to keep expenses variable and cash available. Expenses should only increase when sales do. To achieve this, a new class of worker is being created with effective collaboration now possible over the Internet: the online contingent professional. Fabio Rosati, the CEO of Elance, a leading platform for online employment, says that this newest alternative offers special advantages for small businesses. "At a time of uncertainty, businesses are able to get more work done without having to lose the flexibility and the nimbleness that they need. They are able to find talent very quickly, almost on demand in real time and...pay for either hours they actually worked or results deliverable that are received." In fact, this has become a huge market in the U.S., as a $400 billion piece of the economy with more than 14 million Americans now participating in this type of arrangement.[13]

- **Most importantly, find customers immediately.** Find the prospects that will pay to solve their pain. There is no better funding for a business than paying customers. Investing too much time in product development before customers actually buy the product is a waste of resources and can ultimately lead to the demise of the company when it runs out of cash flow.

The Labor Force: Be Creative

For rural entrepreneurs, training their own people to create the human resources they need is often the only option. In addition, when pioneering a new type of business in an area, entrepreneurs need to do a lot of training. The first manufacturing firm in a community with no history of manufacturing jobs spends a lot of time and money teaching workers how to work in a new way. The first food-processing plant manager in Alva, Oklahoma, had trouble convincing workers that they could not walk in the door at 8 A.M.; they had to be on the line and ready to work at 8 A.M. Then, there was the problem of convincing men that they could run a broom. To the farm guys, that was women's work. So it's not just a matter of teaching technical skills; it also includes soft skills and cultural issues.

Small town businesses have also used technology to creatively get around workforce limits by employing a remote workforce of people that do not live in town. Because technology allows collaboration over great distances, there is no reason to be limited to just the residents of the same geographic area. More information about the remote work trend is found in Chapter 4, "Adapting to the 'Anywhere, Anywhen' Business World."

Being Creative Means Doing Whatever It Takes

Small town business people have a "whatever it takes" attitude. When Becky was a child, her mom and dad owned their own trucking business. One winter, things weren't going great. In fact, things looked bad. They went home to visit their parents in Alva, and cut a big load of firewood while they were there. Then, they headed back to their home in Oklahoma City. They put the firewood out for sale at convenience stores. That wasn't part of their long-term business plan. They weren't going into the firewood business. But, they did have a "whatever it takes" attitude. The firewood sales helped keep their family and the business going through the winter. They turned around the trucking business, and it became the first of many successful businesses.

Big Brand Solutions and Examples

Although brands have traditionally been seen as well-funded, some choose to play by the small town rule: Be creative and spend your brainpower before your dollars. Creativity is something that any brand can apply.

Conserve; Stop Spending for Stupid

One lesson that was learned during the Internet bubble of the 1990s is that it is easy to throw money at problem to try to fix it. Tech startups raised billions of dollars to create products that fixed problems that many of us never knew existed. These resulted in wasteful marketing campaigns, such as the Pets.com ad for more than a million dollars during the Super Bowl in 2000.[14] The startup company sold pet supplies over the web. Its mascot, the sock puppet, appeared not only in its infamous ad, but also the New York Thanksgiving Day Parade. The wasteful spending continued, and $300 million of capital was lost when Pets.com went out of business later that year.

During tough times, frugality has become suddenly popular in the business world. Some companies were frugal long before frugal became cool. The founder of IKEA, Ingavar Kamprad—one of the wealthiest people in the world—instilled a frugal work ethic into his company. He lives well below his means, reportedly driving a 15-year-old Volvo, flying economy, and "encouraging IKEA employees always to write on both sides of a paper." In fact, IKEA has become known for cutting costs throughout its production and passing these savings on to consumers through lower prices. This has allowed IKEA to prosper even during the toughest economic times.[15]

Born in the small town of Kingfisher, Oklahoma, Sam Walton set the tone for the frugal Walmart brand. Its value and "down home" no-nonsense message resonates with consumers all over the world. Walton famously drove an old pickup, long after he could afford any car he wanted. It's a trait that his children have carried on.

Chicago's crowdSPRING is a company that built itself by following small town rules. Co-founders Ross Kimbarovsky and Mike Samson were creative and frugal with their funding. Rather than rent some impressive downtown office, they partnered with a design-development firm, and the deal included a tiny amount of office space. This worked for them for 9 months. Even when their company was more than 3 years old, Mike and Ross were still hands-on, occasionally assembling furniture and taking out the trash. When other startups burned through their entire supply of investor cash, crowdSPRING stuck with being frugal, and it thrived because of it.

Barry was frugal in his own company. In fact, for a long time, new employees would have to build their own desks on their first day of work!

Google has grown with little traditional marketing. It spends less than 1 percent of its revenue on advertising.[16] Ironically, to reach traditional bricks-and-mortar businesses with local advertising, Google uses direct mail, sending businesses credits that they can use on online AdWords purchases.

Growing Slowly, with the Cycles

The smart corporations learn how to be more profitable in down times. By following small town rules, big brands need to be flexible enough to expand and contract with the business cycles. A business typically cycles through these stages in its lifetime, and it may cycle through them more than once because of acquisitions, mergers, and changes in ownership and management.

In the Beginning

Businesses start off with the passions, dreams, and visions of what the founders want it to be.

There is nothing like starting a new business with fresh ideas and an exciting plan. It is similar to the sheer innocence and endless promise of a new baby coming into the world. There is naiveté when starting a business, or it may never get off the ground. Many business founders have said that, if they would have known how hard it would be, they might never have started.

Stuck in the Middle

There is little control here. Business owners at this stage do little choosing and more doing. They look around as broadly as possible at their situation and react. They do whatever comes next based on the results of their last decision. Every decision made is based on incomplete information. No matter how many "facts" are collected, there is no right answer. The only wrong decision is not to make one. At this stage, a key skill is flexibility. Owners must carefully listen to what clients say about the product through their acceptance or rejection of parts of the business. The next step is to evolve and change to meet the clients' needs.

At the End

Although every owner wants to call the ending at their own choosing, most don't. This may be a profitable end of the story where the business is sold. It may be calling it quits because the economics of the business make no sense. Remember that winners know how and when to quit. Hard work and luck may also mean that the business is sold for a large profit.

When businesses expand too fast, it's a symptom of ignoring the cycles. Many companies make the mistake of "growing themselves broke." At one time, Starbucks bragged that in 10 years, it had gone from 1,000 stores to 13,000 stores. In 2009, in response to the economic cycles, the company closed 300 stores and cut thousands of jobs.[17] In 2010, Toyota CEO Akio Toyoda admitted that the company had expanded too fast, resulting in the lowering of quality standards and the deaths of 30 people in the United States.[18]

There are many examples of franchises that expanded too quickly. Krispy Kreme Doughnuts used a blend of marketing and tasty products to create a cult-like following in the early 2000s. When new territories were reached, excited customers would even stand in line to buy its donuts. *Fortune Magazine* named it the hottest brand in 2003. When the company went public and immediately had the money to rapidly expand, the company diluted its status by opening many more locations and distributing its product even further in other stores and gas stations. A few years later, many of the stores were forced to close as the company's profits drastically shrank.

In 1993, after Boston Market went public and had the capital to expand, the company lost sight of its brand, opening up many more locations. The company lost its focus and rapidly expanded its menu. In the late 1990s, the company filed for Chapter 11 bankruptcy and was purchased by McDonalds.[19]

Getting Creative in Tough Times

Business cycles teach companies of all sizes to increase their profitability and seek creative solutions. This happens especially when sales go down and profit needs to remain constant or grow to meet the bottom-line objective.

One of Barry's past clients in Chicago is a $50 million company that has been in business for almost 100 years. Historically, it has delivered only 5 percent net profit to the bottom line of the parent company. Sales have grown slowly over the years, so there was never a need to make any change because the company could predict what it could expect year to year. In 2001, when the business cycle crashed its industry particularly hard, the company was finally forced to make changes. No matter how the company calculated it, a 50 percent drop in sales would mean disaster for its overall profit contribution. The CEO desperately looked for ways to cut expenses or increase gross profit while not cutting revenue. It was able to do this by throwing out established distribution channel assumptions, cutting discounts for many vendors, and raising prices for newer products to its customers.

The company would not have done this if it had not hit a bad economic cycle. As a result, it was able to deliver the same dollar profit to the parent corporation. Now that times are better, and sales have grown again, it can keep the same percent net income and actually raise its contribution to the parent company. Without these cycles, the CEO would have never questioned the basic assumptions of how the business operated and never been able to raise its percentage of contribution to the parent company. Tough times forced it to dig deeper, challenge decade-old assumptions, and find profit that it is now able to take advantage of during the good parts of a business cycle.

In recent years, a model that has become popular during down economic cycles is "reverse auctions." Accepting multiple bids for a project has always been commonplace. But, in this scenario, the buyer asks for bids to do a job or service. Most of the time, this is now done online through a website. Multiple sellers offer bids and, in effect, compete against each other in terms of price or service. As the auction progresses, the prices usually go down as sellers compete to offer lower bids by as much as 20 percent. This was simply not available on a wide-scale or efficient manner before the Internet. Consumer success stories in this area include Lending Tree, which does this with consumer mortgages, and eHealth Insurance, which helps customers find the best health insurance.[20]

Another model that has recently become popular is crowdsourcing, which is where companies outsource various tasks that are usually handled by employees or subcontractors to "the community," asking them to contribute ideas or even do part of the work. This can lower the development costs of products and services. For example, Threadless in Chicago solicits shirt designs from its community and then asks that community to vote on the best ones. The winning designs are sold and sell well, because they are what the community wants to buy!

Summary: Resources Are Now Limited

Businesses are facing tighter lending, lower consumer demand, and a limited supply of skilled workers. These resource limits make the entire business environment much like a small town.

The Small Town Rule: Spend Creative Brainpower Before Dollars

The corollaries:

1. **Conserve.** Make being frugal a way of life.

2. **Be creative in financing.** Instead of seeking more financial resources, seek more creative solutions. Forget traditional

sources, like banks, when there are so many additional ways to find money to grow a business.

3. **Be creative in finding a workforce.** Train a staff locally or find online contingent professionals anywhere in the world that have the needed skills.

4. **Being creative means doing whatever it takes.** Resiliency has always been the hallmark of a successful entrepreneur.

A Look Ahead: Will the Rule Be Relevant Tomorrow?

For the foreseeable future, resources will remain scarce.

Lending will be tight for a long while. New regulations are taking effect. The total potential defaults in residential and commercial lending remain high. Bank consolidations continue, and local control of lending is decreasing.

Consumer demand is volatile, short term or long term. U.S. consumers have shifted away from excessive spending and, as the population ages, they are more likely to save than spend. The squeezing of the middle class is affecting the buying habits of the largest consumer group. This could lower consumer demand for a long time.

The workforce outlook is also tied to the aging population. As the Baby Boomer workforce continues to retire over the next decade, many industries will face more critical workforce shortages.

Being frugal may go in and out of style, but it never loses relevance. When all the "cool kids" are spending money like water, the smart ones are watching every dollar.

Powerhouse Small Town Brands

Viking Range
Greenwood, Mississippi: Population 18,000

Viking Range brought commercial-style ranges to serious home cooks from the heart of the Mississippi Delta. Viking Range founder, Fred Carl, Jr., and his family have lived in Greenwood for generations. Both his father and grandfather were contractors, and Fred grew up in the business. Although his original dream was to be a designer or architect, he instead faced the collapse of his father's business. Fred stepped in and spent a decade rebuilding it.

Fred focused on building contemporary houses with industrial-style kitchens. He ran into a problem: Existing residential stoves were not of the quality that serious cooks wanted, and commercial models simply weren't designed to go in houses safely or affordably.

Fred spent a year and a half perfecting a design that had the look and quality of a commercial model, but without the potential safety problems and the high cost. He took the design to several manufacturers, but none would touch it. He worked with contract manufacturers, but was still not happy with the quality. That left Fred with the option of starting his own manufacturing, which would require substantial upfront capital. He didn't have a product to sell or even show designers, so he had an airbrushed illustration done for a brochure. He went to kitchen designers and built some advance buzz. It took more than 5 years from that first design drawing to the first safety-standard approved prototype. Ultimately, Viking Range took off to national success.

The community of Greenwood has benefitted from more than just the location of the headquarters or manufacturing. Fred has purchased and restored three blocks of downtown buildings. An abandoned downtown hotel was rehabilitated into a boutique hotel. A cooking school draws in Viking Range owners from all around the world. Now, downtown Greenwood thrives with many other businesses, stores, and apartments.

Fred Carl, Jr., followed the small town rules of looking long term to survive the 5 years from idea to product and by investing in his own manufacturing facility. He also used creativity instead of cash when he used illustrations in place of expensive prototypes to build early demand.

"Greenwood is my hometown," Fred said. "It means a lot to me to think I've made a positive economic impact on our community, and I want to help it continue to thrive and grow. Margaret and I have been fortunate because we were always surrounded by good people who believed in this project and who gave me a tremendous amount of encouragement. There is still so much potential for development of new products, and we've shown that it can be done right here in the Mississippi Delta."

3

Adapting to the New Economic Realities of Self-Reliance

When there is no one else to rely on, it's just like a small town. In today's economy, self-reliance has become a requirement. Jobs are no longer assured, incomes are no longer always rising, and the federal or state governments do not offer a reliable backup plan. As these factors increase in importance in the national economy, it follows the pattern that small towns have long since adjusted to.

Small town business people have a sense of self-reliance. They build their own business portfolios with multiple lines of income. Many use online marketplaces to supplement the local marketplace. Brands can adopt diversification as a survival strategy, but it comes with risks. They must consider the possibilities of brand dilution and completely changing their brand through any extensions.

There is no point in waiting around for someone else to help when times get tough. It's up to brands and businesses to survive on their own. This small town rule now applies everywhere, and smart businesses are multiplying their lines of income to diversify their risk.

The Change: No Sure Things (A Job, Income, or Help from the Government)

Getting and keeping a job is no longer a sure thing. The shedding of jobs in the American economy has been dramatic since 2008. More than 7 million jobs have been permanently lost from 2008 through 2010. Entire industries have contracted, requiring fewer workers and providing fewer jobs. All sectors of the economy have been affected, including very different fields like real-estate services, manufacturing, construction workers, retail staff, interior designers, and advertising copywriters. Many predict that it will be at least 5 years before the economy regains these jobs, and it is likely that the new jobs will be in different industries with different job titles than the ones that were lost, which leaves the workforce needing to adjust to the new opportunities.

Long-term unemployment is more common than any time since 1948. As of May 2010, more than 4 percent of the total labor force had been unemployed for 6 months or more.[1] This is a much larger job loss than previous recessions.[2]

Maintaining a household's current income is no longer a sure thing. Even those who did not lose their jobs have found their incomes reduced. In fact, wage cuts have been the topic of strikes and frustration worldwide. American household income numbers dropped dramatically in many of the same regions that realized big increases up through 2007.[3]

Government support is also no longer a sure thing. American confidence in the government in times of crisis took a huge downturn with the televised aftermath of Hurricane Katrina in 2005. The images of people desperate for food and water, stranded in the New Orleans Superdome, left the public wondering who would be there to help in disaster. New York University's Paul C. Light said that Hurricane Katrina "appears to have near-catastrophic impacts on public confidence in the local and federal governments on which they depend for help during emergencies."[4]

A blow to financial confidence in government came from the bailout of banks and auto manufacturers deemed "too big to fail" that ignored the failures of many other businesses, large and small. Now that banks are back to raking in record profits, little of this is going to support loans for a growing economy.

Many state governments are in tough financial shape as a result of years of budget shortfalls. In fiscal years 2009 and 2010, most states saw revenue drops and increasing demand for services. Some states were able to close part of the gaps with funds from the American Recovery and Reinvestment Act. In fiscal year 2011, 46 states reported budget shortfalls. For fiscal year 2012, 39 states projected another year of shortfalls. Cuts to services are expected to continue as states try to balance budgets. Those cuts come even as demand for state-government services increase.[5] People who once thought that they could rely on the government if they got into real trouble have been forced to re-evaluate that way of thinking.

Impact on Brands: No Sure Thing

Even for big brands, survival is no sure thing. There is no assurance of financial support from the parent corporation. There is no guarantee that the industry as a whole will survive.

Since the 1930s, most brands were part of large corporate portfolios. Brand portfolios were managed for economy of scale and efficiencies, while individual brands were allocated their own resources and enough autonomy to be marketed as a separate business. Brands that ran into problems or a down period could get support from profitable brands and "cash cows" in the portfolio. But, in an environment where the entire portfolio of brands may be down, there is no place for the weakest brands to hide.[6] Auto brands that have been cut from corporate portfolios include Saturn and Pontiac. Procter and Gamble (P&G) thinned its portfolio and discontinued the 100-year old Max Factor brand in the United States.

Entire industries have found that there is no sure thing. Newspapers have struggled with the proliferation of competing news and advertising sources. Music labels have been decimated by plummeting sales, as unpaid downloads replace purchased music. Utilities that once enjoyed a regulated monopoly have faced deregulation and competition. No matter how big or how respected the brand, continued success is not a sure thing.

Why Small Town Businesses Survive

In a small town, people have always had to rely on themselves. The typical person in a small town can't count on a job, an income, a loan, or the government.

Because rural people have a sense of self-reliance, they have a feeling of confidence that they can handle whatever comes. This type of confidence and resiliency is a big asset for entrepreneurs.

Job opportunities in small towns have always been limited. In many small towns, the economy is dominated by a single industry or even a single large employer. This includes Winnebago in Forest City, Iowa, and Carnegie Steel in Youngstown, Ohio. Concrete, Washington, was named for the local cement industry. When the last cement plant closed down, the town lost not only the big employer, but also much of its sense of identity. Today, there are "bushel baskets" full of news stories about small towns that lost their one big employer or one big industry.

Incomes are lower in small towns. Per-capita income in rural areas has lagged behind urban and suburban areas for a long time. For example, in 2008, the U.S. median household income was $52,029. Very urban Cook County in Illinois, where Barry lives, had a median household income of $54,559 that same year. In very rural Woods County in Oklahoma, where Becky lives, it was $38,676. This difference of almost 30 percent is significant.

Government services are not easily accessible in many small towns. Although major urban areas have offices for every government service, small town residents may have to drive for several hours to access them. To avoid the travel time, small town people have learned to do without those services whenever possible.

Because they can't count on anything outside, small town people are more likely to start their own business than big city residents. The per-capita rates of self-employment are higher in rural areas. It is estimated that, by 2015, one in four workers in rural America will be self-employed in some capacity.[7]

Beyond self-reliance through self-employment, rural entrepreneurs develop multiple and complementary lines of income to survive. Farmers have done this type of diversification for years within their own operations. Wheat farmers in northwest Oklahoma frequently use the winter wheat as pasture for calves over the winter. Long ago, Becky's great-grandfather would harvest the wheat in the summer, plant cowpeas, let the cattle graze that crop off, and then return the ground for wheat again in the winter. That's three products from one field in a year. Rural entrepreneurs have adapted this farming technique for business to cope with limited local markets. If one local market cannot support a particular line of business to a full-time income level, small town people either start traveling to pick up additional business from other towns or pursue additional business opportunities.

Becky and her husband Joe are perfect examples of this lifestyle. They own a cattle ranch and a liquor store. Becky is also a consultant on small town issues, co-founded an online learning site, and is a professional speaker. That's a broad portfolio, but it is required. The cattle market can take a downturn at any moment. Becky vividly remembers where she was when the first case of Bovine Spongiform Encephalopathy (BSE, or incorrectly "Mad Cow") disease was reported in the United States. Following the announcement, day after day, week after week, the cattle market closed "limit down," taking their year's ranching income down with it. It took several years for the U.S. cattle markets to recover. This kind of volatility is part of the cattle business. If cattle are down, they hope the liquor business will be stable or up.

Donna Maria, the INDIE Business Coach, told her family's story of farmers who used this entrepreneurial spirit to maintain multiple lines of income:

> Consider my maternal grandparents, Sallie and Oren McWilliams. The grandchildren of slaves, they raised five children together on their North Carolina farm. Here are a few of the things they did to create multiple streams of income.
>
> They grew and sold vegetables and tobacco. They leased their land to people who used it to grow and sell crops of their own. They sold eggs from the chicken coop in the back yard. My grandmother made money as a midwife. They sold the pecans that grew on the pecan tree in the front yard (at least the ones my brother and I didn't eat...).
>
> My grandfather was an accomplished builder, and not only did he build his own family's home, but he also contracted workers to help others build their homes and barns. My grandmother canned and sold fruits, vegetables and preserves, and often gave them away to families who had little to eat. She also made and sold clothing.[8]

Bill Burch, founder of Commercial Resources, Inc., is based in Appanoose County, Iowa. It is the 97th poorest of all 99 Iowa counties in per-capita income. He runs 18 businesses, with a total of 150 employees. They include a nursing home, appliance store, restaurant, publishing, manufacturing, property holding, convenience store, and a business services firm that concentrates on operations, accounting and employment-related services. Bill's philosophy is that if the town did not have something he needed, he created it![9]

Kevin and Helen Wiley opened a restaurant in the town of Kinde, Michigan (population 445). In 15 years, they've not only thrived, but they've diversified their lines of income with an ice-cream parlor, miniature golf course, water slide and climbing wall, catering business, and a hall for parties in their small business empire.[10]

Barbara J. Winter, author of *Joyfully Jobless*, talks about building a "Portfolio of Profit Centers." She encourages people to look for multiple ways to generate income from a single basic idea. A musician might do paid performances, lessons, and recordings to generate income, all related to musical knowledge. She relates this back to the creative process, a personal Renaissance.[11]

One creative small town resident is Hugh MacLeod, formerly of Alpine, Texas. He is more frequently found on remote Florida beaches these days, when he's not in Los Angeles or New York on business. He's an artist and cartoonist who also works as a marketing consultant on a global scale. He works with companies as diverse as Microsoft and South Africa's Stormhoek Winery. "It's good to have a lot of different irons in the fire," MacLeod said. "Not just financial reasons, it's just hard to stay interested in the same thing, day after day...."[12]

This idea of multiple lines of work received popular press when the waves of layoffs swept through the U.S. economy in 2008 and 2009. Several experts mentioned the wisdom of the small town rule: Have a side income-producing project to protect yourself should you lose your day job. Small town people have been doing that exact thing for years.

The Small Town Rule: Build Multiple Lines of Income

Building multiple lines of income is the small town answer to the necessity of self-reliance. The supporting corollaries are to know how to manage those multiple lines effectively and take advantage of ways to diversify online.

How to Manage Multiple Lines of Income

Small town businesses thrive by using multiple lines of income. Just like in an investment portfolio, diversity protects them from major downturns. However, managing a diverse portfolio of businesses while still retaining focus can be problematic. Although some businesses fit together as neatly as the wheat-cowpeas-cattle rotation from Becky's great-grandfather, most don't. Successful small town businesses make use of a few common methods to manage these business portfolios successfully.

The first method is to find common themes or consolidate opportunities. Gina Blitstein said on Twitter, "I think of it as a tangle of yarn and if I just pull the right one in the right direction, it will all straighten out and be cohesive."[13] Becky specifically looked for common themes among her consulting businesses. She works with small town governments and nonprofits on grant applications and project management. She helps small tourism businesses and nonprofits with their web presence. With Sheila Scarborough, Becky created a training course related to tourism and social-media marketing. She also publishes Small Biz Survival, about small town business. Becky speaks on small business and social networking, frequently for small town audiences. Exploring all those disparate-seeming projects, she realized the common theme was supporting small town businesses.

The second method is to focus on managing time. With multiple opportunities, prioritizing is how small town business people keep getting things done and keep moving forward. Having a portfolio of projects or opportunities does not mean that all of them must be active at all times. One or two may be active, with other items in the background, waiting to come up when they are ready. Managing diverse businesses also means managing time effectively so focus can be maintained. Becky may start the day working on a deposit for the liquor store, head to the ranch to work calves, answer emails from the field on her smartphone, and then get back to her office to work on a project for a consulting client. By focusing on each one in turn, she keeps them all moving.

The third method is to only build one opportunity at a time. Small town business people focus on one project or line of business. They build it to the point that it requires much less founder input. When they get to this state, they look to the next business to build. This almost always means hiring people and delegating some responsibility. At this stage, it helps to have expert staff in each business that can service the daily customer needs. By building incrementally, entrepreneurs are building in much the same way as Richard Branson built Virgin brands: one opportunity at a time.

There is a downside to maintaining multiple lines of income. Although this technique cuts the risk of total loss, it also cuts the potential return. In an ideal situation, an entrepreneur could find and focus on the single-most profitable opportunity and then maximize that business. Entrepreneurs who laser focus all of their working life on one thing are more likely to create a lasting, meaningful impact in that area.

Author Jonathan Fields asked, "Are you building a body of work, or a cornucopia of chaos?":

> Powerful legacies rarely if ever come in the form of scattershot, piecemeal efforts, cornucopias of chaos," Fields said, "no matter how fun, windswept, or purposeful they seem when we're adrift within them.[14]

Tim Berry, business planning expert, said on Twitter, "There's a lot to be said for cutting the disparate lines and focusing on doing better in the most promising."[15]

Should entrepreneurs diversify to build a portfolio of lines of income, or focus in on one thing only? Small town rules dictate that, in this economy, successful small town businesses diversify to reduce their risk, but they can do so within one unified area of expertise.

Diversifying Online: Selling Expertise

Small town businesses build a portfolio of different income-generating businesses. Transferring that idea to the online world means finding a way to generate income in another marketplace by a different distribution method. Rather than focus on the "Internet" side of the business, successful small town businesspeople start with a teachable skill or a marketable product.

Entrepreneurs who have skills that other people might want to learn can profit by selling what they know online. This comes from the rural tradition of distance learning, long before there was the University of Phoenix. In 1892, Pennsylvania State University took advantage of rural free delivery, called "the 19th Century's version of the Information Highway," to reach rural families with both agricultural knowledge and university courses.[16] Rural areas have taken the lead in adopting other distance-learning techniques at all levels.

In a current example, wedding planner Shayna Walker supplemented her small town wedding-planning company with an online business teaching others the business of wedding planning. When she found the local market too limited and the local social structure hard to break into, she created a resource site for professional wedding planners called Life in Weddings. She is leveraging what she learned as a local expert and is helping others learn and improve their business, regardless of where they are located. She plans to offer books, information products, training, and consulting to other wedding businesses.[17]

Brian Clark and Tony Clark started an online course called "Teaching Sells" to help others learn how to diversify online. The accelerating pace of change in today's business world is driving the need for online education.

> And it's not just business, trade, and financial issues, either (which is a gigantic market)," Brian says. "Think about the demand for personal development training in creativity, productivity, critical thinking communications, and advanced interpersonal skills. This type of training will be as important as substantive and technical information when it comes to being an economically productive person. Add in hobbies, health and wellness, spirituality, coping skills, technology tutorials, parenting issues, and a whole host of things that are right around the corner that we haven't yet imagined and you start to realize how big this is.[18]

This works because the education of customers is central to many businesses. In retail, entrepreneurs are educating many customers about their products or how to use them to solve their pain. Each interaction with a customer is another chance to offer some new learning. In a service business, entrepreneurs are educating clients how better to use their services, or how they can do more themselves. Any media-related business is basically an information-sharing service that educates the reader.

Some entrepreneurs find it intimidating to offer education or training online. However, many of them are already offering some local education. Examples of small businesses offering training are everywhere. The Alva Sewing Center offers classes in sewing and quilting, from beginners to advanced learners. Becky's mother Glenna Mae Hendricks teaches local wine-tasting classes. A camera-store owner in Enid, Oklahoma, offers beginner classes to customers in how to use their new camera. It's not that much more difficult to take the education that small businesses are already offering in informal ways and create a more formal online offering.

Teaching online can be done many different ways. The product can be a paid newsletter or eBook. Instruction can be done through webinars (web seminars) or online courses made up of several lessons.

There are differences in distance learning and in-person learning. By using text descriptions, photos, audio instructions, and video demonstrations, entrepreneurs can teach almost anything. Educational research has established that distance learning can be as effective as in-person learning. The key factors are to use the right methods for the tasks, provide student-to-student interaction, and give timely feedback from teachers to students.[19]

Online learning tools can excel at providing that student interaction. Online forums let people interact with text, building threaded conversations. In fact, online forums have been around so long, almost everyone online has used one. Plug-in forum software allows almost any website or blog to include a forum.

Instant messaging provides an effective back-and-forth conversation with one individual or groups. Most instant-messaging services also have added video interaction. Other services allow audio interaction with students and broadcasts of teaching material. Any kind of website can be used as the base of a learning-based business. There are also learning/teaching platforms that have already been built, which are included in Appendix A, "Resources for Implementing the Small Town Rules."

Market Online to Diversify

An online business can be used as a tool to better market an existing business. Entrepreneurs can reach out far beyond geographic boundaries. VPG Printing was just another local printer until Laura Beulke went online offering specials and making friends on Twitter. She began by offering advice on printing services. She tried sharing special rates on Twitter, but the thing that really took off was "freebies." Beulke didn't give away huge services, just a little bit of printing or a product as a freebie. But that snowballed as people began to retweet and share her free offers. She picked up hundreds of new followers. Beulke added clients in 15 states and doubled the number of states where VPG Printing does business through marketing online with Twitter.[20]

Big Brand Solutions: Extending Brands for Survival

Economic, technological, and societal changes have forced big brands to adapt. The small town rule of creating multiple lines of income can be a problem for brands that succeed best by focusing on one thing across geographic boundaries. But, knowing that markets can shift out from under them and needing to plan for the long term, brands have to make smart moves into new products or lines following the small town rule to build one line at a time: establish first, then extend.

When does a brand extension become a brand dilution instead? It's largely a matter of hindsight. If it succeeds, it's a brand extension; if it fails, the term is dilution.

Small town rules dictate that a successful business should only expand one line at a time, establishing the primary brand first. The management team should only "sell what they know." Then, it is smart to add additional lines of business after there is a sufficient foundation to build on. This is the same pattern farmers use to establish multiple crops: Make sure the primary crop is working well, then add side crops one at a time to the farm. Virgin Brands, Zappos, and Amazon have all used the same small town rule.

Virgin Brands might be the most studied of all brands, and maybe the most diverse. It seems whatever strikes the fancy of Virgin co-founder Richard Branson is fair game, but the diversification actually follows the small town rule for brands that first establish, then extend. Virgin Records began as a mail-order record retailer in 1970, then grew into a record shop, then established a recording studio in just a few years. Now, the Virgin Group includes 200 companies across 30 countries.

How did Branson create such a broad palette of brands? Gradually. He built around his driving force, finding new ways to help people have a good time in unexpected places. That translates into the idea of the Virgin brand, one that is more about the experience than about the company.

Following the small town rule, Branson credits Virgin's gradual development and diversification for how it has been able to survive during the recession. He proudly points out that Virgin is the only one of the top 20 brands to have diversified so broadly, with more billion-dollar companies in more sectors than any other company.

"As a result of this diversification, Virgin has been able to weather the storm of the recession," Branson said. "Our risks are spread over many companies, industries, and countries; the failure of one will not bring down the whole group."[21]

One notable failure was when Branson launched Virgin Cola in the 1990s to compete with Coke and Pepsi. For the launch, in typical Branson over-the-top publicity style, he rode a Sherman tank through New York's Times Square to fire at the Coca-Cola billboard. He was taking on the brand giants, but Virgin could not win the distribution war with Coke and Pepsi, and it eventually failed.[22]

Both Zappos and Amazon have been able to successfully make brand extensions for their online retail companies. Both started by establishing a core competence in a single line of retail products, using the small town rule of establish, then extend. Although Amazon started out as an online book store, it now sells many different lines of business, from music to lawn mowers. Zappos successfully expanded from selling shoes online to clothes, accessories, and many other items. Both companies revolutionized the online retail industry. Amazon was seen as a prophet of the potential of online retail long before any other brands believed in it. Zappos turned "free shipping both ways" into a weapon, forcing other retailers to adapt. In 2009, Amazon acquired Zappos, extending Amazon's brand into the customer-centric world of Zappos.

Many big brands even extend so far that they totally "morph" their business so it is unrecognizable from its origins. Nokia started out selling rubber tires and boots. Nintendo was a playing card company. Ben and Jerry first looked into bagels, not ice cream. Raytheon got started in refrigerator manufacturing; today, it's a military contractor.

Sometimes, companies are forced to exit businesses entirely. At one time, there were more than 2 million payphones in the U.S. Today, after the major corporations like AT&T and Verizon have exited the business (remember cell phones?), there are now only 700,000.[23]

The wheel of retailing theory says that as existing businesses become long established, they continue to add additional services and selection, broadening out from the initial focus. Then, they become vulnerable to upstart companies with lower prices, fewer services and tighter, more focused offerings. This natural cycle of older brands being undercut by newer discount brands has led many companies to start their own discount brand.

Better to be undercut by a brand within the same corporate group than by someone outside.

With the success of discount airline Southwest, many other companies tried to start their own discount brand within their corporate portfolio. For United, the TED brand was created in 2004. It was not the core management team's expertise, and the company folded back into United in 2008. Hertz took a different approach when it acquired Advantage Rental Car in 2009 to serve as its discount brand.

McDonald's, once a fast-food hamburger, fries, and milkshake place, started to serve breakfast with the introduction of the Egg McMuffin in 1972 by one of its franchisors. Breakfast is now a key part of its business. Not all brand experiments succeed, however. In 1996, McDonald's created the Arch Deluxe. It was supposed to extend McDonald's brand to more adult-themed menu items. The company spent $100 million on the ad campaign. Arch Deluxe was supposed to earn $1 billion in sales its first year, but it was priced too high and failed.

As another example, in 1993, Burger King introduced waiters as part of its dining experience. During the hours of 5 P.M. to 8 P.M., customers could have their meal served to them at their table. It was not valuable for most customers, and it was discontinued a short time afterwards.[24]

Many brands have tried to extend out from their core competence into a completely new line of business. Many examples did not go well, such as Dunkin' Donuts bagels (why buy a bagel when a dozen donuts will do?), Bic pen underwear (disposable underwear?), Ben-Gay aspirin (no one wants to swallow a Ben-Gay product), Colgate kitchen entrees (its toothpaste tastes good, but should we eat it?), Life Savers soda (anyone for drinking liquid candy?), Frito-Lay lemonade (its products make consumers thirsty), Cosmopolitan yogurt (not sexy enough), and Smith and Wesson bicycles (OK, they are both made of metal).[25]

Summary: No Sure Things (A Job, Income, or Help from the Government)

Uncertainty is the main characteristic of the economy and society today. It extends to jobs, personal incomes, and even entire industries. In times of crisis, most people no longer think they can rely on help from the government. To survive, individuals, businesses and brands must be more self-reliant, just like small town businesses and people.

The Small Town Rule: Multiply Lines of Income to Diversify Your Risk

Building multiple lines of income is the small town answer to the necessity of self-reliance.

The corollaries:

1. **Start your own business, at least on the side.** Every person now needs a backup plan. Individuals can explore interests on the side that may become an income-generating opportunity if they lose their job. Brands can consider brand extensions that help diversify the risk.

2. **Manage multiple lines of income.** Find common themes or consolidate opportunities. Find complementary ways to make money that prosper in different economic cycles.

3. **Focus on managing time.** With multiple businesses or income streams, time management and focus become critical for success.

4. **Build one opportunity at a time.** Target building one business at a time until employees can be hired to execute daily tasks.

5. **Diversify online.** Extend your company by selling expertise about your business.

A Look Ahead

Looking into the future, there is no sure thing. Although the general job market will likely improve in the next few years, the outlook for any individual is less certain. The loyalty between employer and employee is broken on both sides. Income levels may rebound, but they will remain susceptible to new threats and uncertainties in the global economy. Governments at all levels are far too busy with their own crises to help any individual business out.

That leaves smart entrepreneurs and brands to follow the small town rule: Self-reliance beats the alternative.

Powerhouse Small Town Brands

Walmart

Bentonville, Arkansas: Population 35,000

The most powerful small town brand is also the most controversial: Walmart. Founder Sam Walton grew up during the Depression, in a series of small towns in Oklahoma and Missouri. He learned the discount-retail business with Ben Franklin stores in the 1950s. In 1962, he opened his first Wal-Mart Discount City store in Rogers, Arkansas, which had a population of about 5,700 at the time. Headquarters were established in nearby Bentonville, Arkansas.

Wal-Mart Stores, Inc., now has 8,900 locations in 30 countries worldwide under 55 different names and revenue of more than $400 billion per year, with an estimated 2 million employees. In addition to retail stores, it has diversified into logistics, real estate, insurance claims management, and financial services firms. It is the world's 18th largest public corporation, and the headquarters are still in Bentonville. As Walmart has grown, so has Bentonville, from 3,700 in 1960 to more than 35,000 in 2010.

Throughout its history, Walmart kept small town values of thrift and friendliness. Among its many awards, it was named one of the top ten retailers in *Fortune Magazine*'s 2010 Most Admired Companies survey.

The other side of the story is how Walmart reshaped small towns, devastating downtown merchants. Kenneth Stone, professor of economics at Iowa State University, compared the effect of Walmart to other negative forces on small town retail, including railroads, mail-order catalogs from Sears Roebuck and Montgomery Ward, and shopping malls.

Does the number of jobs created at Walmart equal the number destroyed in independent retail and manufacturing? Do the low-price savings for the average working family make up for the low wages of Walmart's own jobs and the economic incentives granted by local government? How much does the siphoning of profits to corporate headquarters hurt the local economy of thousands of small towns?

There is no doubt that Walmart is a powerhouse brand that grew from Sam Walton's small town beginnings and is still based in a small town today. It thrived by following many of the small town rules, including diversifying its income streams from a single discount store to 55 different store names and many supporting services.

"There is only one boss. The customer. And he can fire everybody in the company from the chairman on down, simply by spending his money somewhere else," Sam Walton said.

"Each Wal-Mart store should reflect the values of its customers and support the vision they hold for their community."

4

Adapting to the "Anywhere, Anywhen" Business World

Geographic advantage used to be a key driver in business. As many big-city businesses find themselves losing their geographic advantage, it's similar to when small towns lost their geographic advantage in previous eras.

Physical goods can be shipped anywhere globally. Downloadable information can be delivered electronically almost instantly. Many services can be provided using communication tools, regardless of location.

Brands have been affected by this new geography, and jobs are no longer tied to one physical location. Working remotely is fast becoming a business imperative.

Small towns offer a good model for adapting to the loss of geographic advantage. The changes brought to small towns by railroads and interstate highways foreshadowed the current changes big-city businesses face. The adoption of smartphones by farmers provides a parallel for big businesses having to adopt new communication technology.

Businesses that once depended on all of their employees to be in the same place working the same hours are now adapting to this new climate. Working remotely is changing the location, and anytime communication is changing the hours. Broadband Internet access disrupts many parts of the business game. Companies are redefining how they see their corporate headquarters in a world where location and time are less restrictive.

The Change: Geographic Advantage Is Shrinking, and Competition Is Everywhere

Throughout history, geography has been one center of business advantage. Craftspeople wanted to be located near raw materials. Farmers wanted the most productive land. Merchants had to be on the trade routes. A navigable harbor became a desirable port. Everyone needed access to drinking water.

In the industrial revolution, sources of power for production were primary advantages. In modern times, transportation and trade have driven geographic advantage. Being on the main highway or near shipping facilities gave a business a geographic advantage over competitors. Distance meant time, and time meant cost or some form of money. People gathered into villages, towns, and ultimately cities around many and any of these things. Jobs were clustered in urban areas where most businesses were.

One major loss of geographic advantage came from the spread of the telephone. In 1880, *Scientific American* magazine described how it was re-organizing society:

> One year, it was a scientific toy with infinite possibilities of practical use; the next it was the basis of a system of communication the most rapidly expanding, intricate, and convenient that the world has known.

> The result can be nothing less than a new organization of society—a state of things in which every individual, however secluded, will have at call every other individual in the community, to the saving of no end of social and business complications, of needless goings to and fro, of disappointments, delays, and a countless host of those great and little evils and annoyances which go so far under present conditions to make life laborious and unsatisfactory. The time is close at hand when the

> scattered members of civilized communities will be as closely
> united, so far as instant telephonic communication is concerned,
> as the various members of the body now are by the nervous
> system.[1]

Today, former geographic advantages are being wiped away. Fast transportation of physical goods reaches most populated parts of the world effi-
ciently. The introduction of containerized intermodal shipping eliminated
many kinds of geographic advantage, making global commerce much less
expensive and much less difficult. It reduced freight costs and remade the
entire industry of moving goods overland and by sea. For businesses, it
reduced inventory costs and decreased the time needed to get any item to
market.[2]

Shippers of consumer products such as UPS and FedEx have changed the
entire game for retailers. Competition is everywhere now. A small company located anywhere can ship packages directly to customers worldwide.
Distribution of goods can still be a political issue in a given country, but
seldom a geographic issue. Today, UPS and the postal service will pick up a
package from Becky's small town and take it anywhere in the world. (However, the nearest FedEx drop box is 50-some miles away.)

One political issue related to distributing goods across the country is sales
tax. Each U.S. state has its own rules about what goods are subject to sales
tax, and at what rates, and what is exempt. This creates enormous difficulties for merchants shipping all across the country, knowing what is taxable
and what is not and at what rate in each different town, city, county, and
state. So far, the solution has been for merchants to claim that they are
exempt and not collect or submit local and state taxes. Online merchants
that ignore sales tax gain a price advantage over local merchants that collect
sales tax. The price difference without sales tax can be more than 10 percent in many locations. That price advantage for online retailers is another
factor eroding the former geographic advantage of local retailers.

As more commerce has gone online, state governments have started trying to collect some of the taxes that are being skipped. Some states, such
as Oklahoma, started requiring all residents to report and pay "use tax" in
place of the sales tax on all goods they buy from out-of-state vendors.

Through the Internet, electronic delivery of goods or services requires
no shipping. RSS feeds using tools like Google Reader let customers pick

up information by their schedule and take it with them. Barry's son once suggested that he could get a toy via the Internet if "the cable got wide enough!"

Impact on Brands and Big Business

The development of national brands contributed to destroying local geographic advantages, and the loss of geographic advantage is now coming home to many national brands and other big businesses.

Loss of geographic exclusivity is one factor behind the failure of many large newspapers. Media writer Jeffrey S. Klein said that, although there are many reasons for their downfall, the loss of geographic exclusivity doesn't get enough attention. At one time, print newspapers were the only local source for formally communicating the news, editorial content, and advertising. Cable television and the Internet ended that local monopoly, bringing news and advertising directly from producers to consumers, wherever they were located.[3]

Jobs are also no longer geographically tied. Many big brands used to locate their large manufacturing facilities in smaller towns because the workforce was non-union and, therefore, the brand could expect to have lower costs and increased flexibility in its largest cost: payroll. The employees were also more loyal because there were limited jobs in the community.

Containerized intermodal shipping also contributed to moving jobs around the country and the world. Some big businesses had tied their factories to existing ports and population centers. With cheaper and more streamlined transportation systems for goods, businesses were able to look to more distant locations and specialized plants. Stages of manufacturing could be split between different factories, with partially finished goods shipped between them.[4]

A large corporation coming into a small town with a new manufacturing or distribution plant could have significant leverage with the local political establishment, including possible tax breaks. This kind of debate has happened in so many real towns, it's now the subject of a movie. In the 2010 movie *Main Street*, a representative of a big company comes to a small town offering jobs for storing toxic waste. There is a debate among the residents on how much this dying town with high unemployment needs this type of business.[5]

Over the past several decades, the low cost of labor in small towns wasn't able to compete against the global low cost of labor, and many brands moved their manufacturing outside of the U.S. But, workers are the ones taking the next step in the loss of geographic advantage.

When work is no longer tied to a specific location, then employees are also no longer tied to a location. The act of working from any location has been given several different labels: Telework, remote work, and work-shifting are some of the most common terms.

For many information workers, working remotely is "fast becoming not a perk, but a business imperative," the website Small Business Trends reported. A Microsoft study, "Work Without Walls," showed that workers want to work remotely to avoid commuting, achieve better work-life balance, and be more productive than they can be in the office. This gives big brands more choice in sourcing the best employees and has the tendency to drive down the cost of such a resource, if the business is ready to support remote working. Still, most companies lack a formal "telework" policy, and 30 percent of the workers in the survey reported that their bosses were actively *not* supporting remote work.[6]

Realizing that technology now pushes the blurring of work and home life, the U.S. Department of Labor has made workplace flexibility a priority issue, hosting a White House Forum and National Dialogue on Workplace Flexibility.[7]

How Small Towns Gave Up Geographic Advantage Long Ago

The loss of geographic advantage is nothing new for small town business owners. They lost their geographical advantages a long time ago with transcontinental railroads and interstate highways. This was decades before overnight air freight or the Internet made distance practically irrelevant, even in major urban centers.

When the interstate highway system connected America in new ways, many small towns found themselves simply bypassed by travelers with money to spend. It was a reminder of the days when railroads could make or break towns and when entire towns would pull up stakes and move to suit the railroads' preferred routes. Small town businesses had to learn to survive a new geographic reality, one where their previous advantage was wiped out. In fact, many have managed to compete globally, even from relatively remote locations, including Walmart, L.L. Bean, Viking Range, Longaberger Baskets, Winnebago, and Grasshopper Mowers. These powerfully successful small town companies are profiled in this book.

With improvements in broadband Internet technology over the last decade, small town stores now can compete with other businesses online, worldwide. This also leads to a commoditization of products.

The home-town bookstore has to face Amazon.com. Many customers will go to the bookstore and then see whether Amazon carries the same book, sometimes from their smartphone while they are actually standing in the local bookstore. Barry's common practice when he finds a product for sale from a specialty retailer is to see whether Amazon sells it. If it does, he would much rather buy this product (because it is then a commodity) from Amazon to take advantage of the free shipping and his trust in this online company. Becky's local liquor store must contend with Wines.com in a similar way for many premium wine sales.

It's not just products. Services have also become a commodity. The small town bookkeeper is up against Mint.com for personal and business accounting. The local designer has to face commodity-crowdsourced designs. Even local advertising has become a commodity with free ads through Craigslist covering some very small towns. This trend will only continue over the next decade, as Internet connectivity becomes ubiquitous and all businesses face the exact same challenge as small town businesses have for decades.

Jim Whitt, author of *Riding for the Brand* and *The Transformational Power of Purpose*, describes how the most rural of businesses, livestock auctions, dealt with the loss of geographic advantage years ago. Back when most cattle sold at livestock auctions or in private trades, a new way of selling cattle started creating buzz. Cattle were videoed and auctioned using a satellite feed.

"The primary advantage was that distance was eliminated," Whitt said. "Instead of traveling to live auctions, you could sit in front of a television and buy cattle regardless of where they were located."

Most local auction owners looked at the satellite auctions as competition. Kenny Sherrill, owner of the Union Stockyards in McAlester, Oklahoma, decided to acquire the franchise for the satellite auction in his area.

Whitt asked Sherrill if he thought the satellite would be the way most cattle would be sold in the future.

"I don't know," Sherrill answered. "But if it is, I'd rather be part of it than having to compete against it."[8]

Like the livestock auctions, farmers depend on information. Farmers have a significant portion of their assets tied up in tangible commodities, like live cattle or grain. They often trade in commodities and futures to protect their investment. In the 1980s and 1990s, some farmers subscribed to special satellite data feeds to receive live commodity prices. The real-time information gave them an advantage in commodity trading, but the desktop terminals weren't mobile. Leaving the office meant losing that information advantage. As soon as smartphone technology arrived, many farmers were quick adopters so they could get their hands on commodity price apps. With them, farmers could keep up with prices and execute trades no matter where they were working. Almost half of farmers in a 2011 Agriculture. com survey use their cell phone to send and receive email and access the Internet from anywhere.[9] Now, iPads and other tablets are adding richer information and better pricing data, not to mention larger display screens, to smart farmers' mobile offices.

The Small Town Rule: Work "Anywhere, Anywhen" Through Technology

Small town businesses have turned the loss of geographic advantage into an opportunity, just like the farmers using iPads to make their offices out in the field. The always-on nature of business today means that people can communicate or collaborate at different times, which is what social business expert Chris Brogan calls "anywhen."

Broadband Internet Makes Working Anywhere Possible

In a 2010 Zogby International survey, people rated the technological developments of the last decade. High-speed Internet was the change that had the greatest impact on people's lives, and it was the one thing they didn't want to live without.[10]

Broadband access in small towns and rural areas varies by location. Availability has improved significantly since 2000, when only the most populated urban areas had broadband access. By 2011, more than 80 percent of the rural U.S. population had access to broadband service.[11] Becky lives in a town of only 30 people, but she uses DSL broadband. If she lived just one mile outside of town, her telephone cooperative could only offer her its much slower dial-up service. Improved access has made it possible for many successful small town entrepreneurs to adopt broadband Internet as a competitive advantage.

Bill Burch, who owns many small businesses in rural Iowa, says, "The Internet makes most everything possible for me. It is the ultimate tool to reach out beyond your local limits and do more. There is nothing I need that I can't find on the Internet. There is nothing I need to know that I can't learn on the Internet. There are very few I can't reach on the Internet."[12]

Jason Kintzler is the founder and CEO of Pitch Engine, a social-media news release firm based in Wyoming. Kintzler says he runs the most remote web 2.0 startup in the lower 48 states of the U.S. A small town guy, cowboy, and CEO, Kintzler has used broadband extensively in building his startup and in promoting his home state. Pitch Engine is now a global company, with customers all across the U.S., Asia, and the Pacific.

"Anywhen" Makes Time-Shifting as Valuable as Work-Shifting

Social-business expert and CEO of Human Business Works Chris Brogan uses the term "anywhen" to describe the time-shifting of work, allowing people to communicate even though the two sides of the conversation may happen at different times. Chris says the telephone solved the problem of anywhere. Two people could communicate no matter where they were, but it required both people to participate at the same time. The Internet solved the problem of "anywhen." With email and online tools, two people could do business anytime and from anywhere. Groups of people could communicate using email without needing everyone to participate at the same time. With social networks and online tools, groups could collaborate on work without working the same hours. Time-shifting becomes just as important as work-shifting to enhancing productivity.[13]

One technology company picked up on the challenge Chris issued. Away-Find sorts through incoming email, finds the urgent messages, then forwards them by voice or by text message, or delegates the messages to another person. The idea is to keep "anywhen" workers from having to be tied to an email inbox and allow them to time-shift most messages to the time the worker chooses. AwayFind CEO Jared Goralnick said that time-shifting is much more possible when combining its tool with appointment scheduling, collaborative writing, and project management tools instead of relying solely on email.[14]

The global economy means more people working in more time zones. Grant Griffiths' startup, Headway Themes, LLC, is based in Clay Center, Kansas (population 4,300). The support team is based across the U.S., France, and Australia. By having support people in all different time zones, they can respond to users almost anytime. The team members have also had to learn to work with each other without being in the same time zone.

Putting It All Together to Be Location Independent

Because business is no longer tied to geographic location, people are moving to where they want to work. The 24/7 pace of the Internet means they can also work when they want to work. These "location-independent" professionals are beginning to value culture and place more than proximity to big employers. These values and how they fit into their personal lifestyles move to the top of the list when evaluating any location, after the speed of the broadband.

Hugh MacLeod, the creative marketing consultant mentioned in Chapter 3, "Adapting to the New Economic Realities of Self-Reliance," has lived in London, New York City, rural Scotland, and Alpine, Texas. Today, he spends time on beaches in Florida, working remotely. Through all those moves, he has kept the same profession and built a global client base.

"In my line of work, you don't need to live in the big city," MacLeod says. "You just need to live near a good airport."[15]

In fact, small town businesses were among the first to use technology to overcome distance. From the small Talisker Distillery on the Isle of Skye in Scotland, huge kegs of Scotch whisky are bound for distribution around the world. The only methods of transportation are by ship from the tiny dock and a winding one-lane road. Yet, Talisker Whisky has been a popular brand worldwide for a few hundred years.

Modern small town businesses use new techniques to overcome distance. Hopunion, LLC, in Washington State distributes locally grown hops to craft brewers all over the world. Using FedEx distribution, it managed to pioneer the delivery of still-green "wet" hops across the country in 48 hours. That let craft brewers and even hobbyists try fresh hop ale styles not previously possible because of the distance from hops growers. It's a loss of geographic advantage for the brewers closest to the growers, and a win for the "anywhere" style of doing business today.[16]

It can take some time to change a local business into an "anywhere" business. When freelance writer Judy Dunn chose to move to an island only reachable by ferry, she converted her writing business from relying on local customers to working remotely. She was able to keep some of her existing customers, but others were not comfortable with her lack of physical presence. They were used to having in-person meetings to discuss writing projects with Judy. She simply had to give up those customers and find new ones. Judy said:

> We found it a very good strategy to start weeding out the "old-fashioned" clients who need a sit-down, in-person meeting for every project, Now, we "pre-screen" to make sure the clients we take on are comfortable with online relationships. We are (fondly) saying good-bye to some, but, at the same time, attracting new ones who are a better fit.

> With all the challenges, it's still worth it living on this gorgeous island on Puget Sound![17]

Aliza Sherman has worked in several rural locations, as she followed her husband's career as a wildlife biologist. She lived several years in Montana, three years in Anchorage, and now lives in Tok, Alaska, with a population around 1,400. When it gets to be –60° Fahrenheit, and there is snow stacked up measured in feet rather than inches, Aliza is still online, working for clients all over the world.

She is a writer and marketer who calls her work "totally portable." Internet connectivity was her first hurdle. DSL access was seven times more expensive in Tok than in Anchorage. She had to try "cobbling together" DSL with an Internet card for her MacBook laptop.[18] Still, she managed to maintain and build her company and now focuses on marketing through mobile technology. She remains in demand on the technology-speaking circuit, making several sojourns a year from Tok to maximize her travel time.

In Australia, the trend of city people moving from the metropolitan areas out to the small towns on the coast for better quality of life was appropriately called a "sea change."

"Increasingly, the urban sophisticates are not necessarily urban," entrepreneur Des Walsh said.

He made his "sea change" long ago. Today, Des operates a number of businesses from his relatively small town of Tweed Heads (population 51,000) on the Gold Coast of Australia.

Scott Jordan moved his business from Chicago, IL, to Ketchum, ID (population 3,000). He wanted to ski in Sun Valley more often. He and his wife, Laura, loved the outdoors and felt that the urban life of Chicago city living stifled them too much. So, eight years ago, he picked up his successful travel clothing business, Scottevest, and moved to Sun Valley. The warehouse and shipping are outsourced to a firm in Chicago, but all the other functions are in Ketchum.

Sturgis, South Dakota, (population 6,600) is a new focus for the firearms-manufacturing industry, with several businesses moving into town. Norma Allen, co-founder of Dakota Arms, said:

> The work ethic of our employees in Sturgis has been outstanding. The move to South Dakota where we have no corporate income tax, no personal income tax, no personal property tax, no inventory tax, and no inheritance tax certainly helps the bottom line in any business. When you make a profit in South Dakota, you get to keep it.[19]

With technology, coworkers no longer have to be in the same room to work together. Tools like Basecamp from 37 Signals and GoToMeeting from Citrix have made working together over long distances virtually seamless. In fact, when Becky and Barry wrote this book, they got together in person only a few times and mostly co-wrote the book through Google Docs and DropBox.

Digital Distribution Extends Reach

The book *Free* by Chris Anderson tells how the cost of digital distribution has dropped to the point it is almost too cheap to measure. This means that producers of any content that can be distributed digitally have a very low barrier to get their products to consumers. It also means that, more often, the digital content is offered for free, with profit coming from another follow-on source. These other revenue streams can be ads in the content or profit from future "up sales" to those same customers. It can be a "freemium" model, where customers get a certain amount for free, but some choose to pay for a more premium product or service.

A business that relies on digital distribution can be located almost anywhere. Only 10 years ago, it made more sense to distribute even a modest amount of data by putting it on a CD and mailing it. Today, customers are more likely to say, "Just DropBox it to me." This is seen in the way that Netflix and Blockbuster are moving away from mailing DVDs to having the movies downloaded to computers or digitally streamed to big-screen televisions.

Forget Outsourcing, Think "Rural Sourcing"

Turning the disadvantage of a rural location into an advantage of lower cost, rural sourcing captures jobs that otherwise might be outsourced overseas. Rural service firms claim a number of advantages over global firms: shorter supply chains, better data security, intellectual property protection, cultural compatibility, and convenient time zones. Costs are lower than traditional urban firms, reflecting the lower rural cost of living.

Firms like Rural Sourcing, Inc., Rural America OnShore Outsourcing, Cross USA, and Onshore Technology are at the forefront of smashing the old geographic disadvantage. This is not a new phenomenon. Saturn Systems, another rural sourcing firm, has been around for more than 20 years. For the first time, the 2011 Gartner Outsourcing and Vendor Management Summit included a pavilion for rural sourcing, showing that this trend is gaining plenty of global attention.

Applying the Small Town Rule to Big Brands

Working for a big brand used to mean that an employee had to be physically located in one of their geographic locations. With small town rules, employees and other independent contractors can now be located anywhere in the world. Technology now allows seamless collaboration over long distances for any employee. For example, Fabio Rosati, CEO of Elance, said that while the corporate office is located in California, the company's receptions function is located in Virginia.[20] Playboy Enterprises' headquarters remain in Chicago, but most of the corporate executives live in California.

In fact, Lenovo, the computer company that bought IBM's ThinkPad line years ago, does not have a world headquarters. Its CEO William Amelio said that great ideas come from everyone around the world, so why would they pick one place to have their headquarters? He works out of many offices by using video conferencing.[21]

Employees no longer have to physically move their families to advance in the company. (Remember how some people called IBM "I've Been Moved?") Online collaboration also gives big brands more flexibility in hiring when they want people and where they want them. Rosati's Elance helps big companies access a flexible workforce of "online contingent professionals."[22] This not only saves big brands lots of money, but more importantly, it allows corporations to focus on hiring the right resource instead of just the right geographic location. It also allows employees and contractors the location and work hour flexibility they may want.

When *Fortune Magazine* publishes its annual list of the 100 Best Companies to Work For, it evaluates perks and benefits. One benefit it tracks is telecommuting. Since 2007, the number of firms on the list offering telecommuting or remote work options has been more than 80 percent.[23]

Companies like Deloitte, Intel, Accenture, and Cisco have more than 80 percent of their staff as regular telecommuters. Many large corporate call centers have been placed in other countries where costs are less and the time shift is important for consumers calling after work in the U.S. Others are turning to rural sourcing firms to place call centers in small towns in the U.S.

One downside of all this is that, for many corporate employees, work hours have become 24/7. Because the corporate smartphone is never far from hand, the expectation for an immediate reply to any request is high. There is always the fear of missing something in the fast-paced connected world.

One startup that has recognized the potential of the small town rule to work anywhere and "anywhen" is Chicago-based crowdSPRING. Its crowdsourcing model relies on the contributions of many location- and time-independent designers rather than using a few in-house designers all located in the same building working the same hours.

> The truth is that a great idea can come from anyone, anywhere—whether they're a janitor by day and a designer by night or a stay-at-home mom who doesn't have the time to run her own web studio. crowdSPRING makes geography and title irrelevant and, thereby, opens new markets for creativity all the world over.[24]

Summary: Geographic Advantage Is Shrinking, and Competition Is Everywhere

Geographic location used to be a key to competitiveness. Now, digital distribution and online collaboration are making geography irrelevant. Small towns dealt with similar blows to geographic advantage in the past, so small town businesses offer an example all business can learn from.

The Small Town Rule: Work "Anywhere, Anywhen" Through Technology

Live where you want. There no longer is a barrier. Go ahead: work anywhere and anywhen.

The corollaries:

1. **Take advantage of broadband**. Fast Internet access is the one utility that is now required for any small business anywhere.

2. **"Anywhen" makes time-shifting as valuable as work-shifting.** Serving customers across the world is now a 24/7 requirement.

3. **Be location independent.** Any small business owner can now live and work where she wants. Time and place are flexible. Any entrepreneur can select the location that best suits his lifestyle, business, family, or preferences. Geography is no longer the barrier to distribution.

4. **Use digital distribution to extend your reach.** Digital distribution is becoming too cheap to measure, allowing businesses to distribute information widely at low cost.

5. **Forget outsourcing, think rural sourcing.** Because a workforce can be anywhere, businesses can reduce costs by using resources that are in more affordable areas of the country.

A Look Ahead

The business world can't turn back from anywhere and "anywhen." Current initiatives to spread broadband access are being joined by projects to increase the understanding and usage of online access. Broadband will become as common as any other power utility. Technology is forcing the merging of business and professional lives, with a 24/7 business cycle. We also "fear" that Barry's son is not far off from getting his toy delivered electronically through a really big Internet cable.

Powerhouse Small Town Brands

L.L. Bean
Freeport, Maine: Population 7,800

L.L. Bean catalogs and stores have brought the Maine outdoors lifestyle to an audience around the world, without ever leaving home.

There really was a man named L.L. Bean: Leon Leonwood Bean. He started his company in 1912 to sell waterproof hunting boots. He was a hunter himself, so he knew what worked in the field. His brother had a clothing store in Freeport Corner, in Freeport, Maine, so L.L. used the basement to start his mail-order business. He quickly hit a setback: 90 of the first 100 pairs of his original production proved defective and were returned. He made good on the money-back guarantee for every pair. Then, he fixed the design and kept going.

Today, L.L. Bean is a $1.5-billion international powerhouse, with stores in China, Japan, and the U.S. It's still based in Freeport, Maine.

From its roots as an outdoors company, L.L. Bean maintained a commitment to environmental stewardship. The corporation builds all new buildings according to the U.S. Green Building Council's LEED certification program, uses alternative fuels in its fleet of vehicles, recycles extensively, and considers environmental impacts from production, marketing, and distribution of its products. The company has a particular interest in the Appalachian Trail, which runs right through Maine. For more than 30 years, L.L. Bean employees have volunteered to maintain a section of the trail, and the corporation has donated to support land acquisition and expansion of stewardship programs.

L.L. Bean followed the small town rules of surviving adversity and economic hardship, treating customers as community, and maintaining strong ties to the local culture. "A customer is the most important person ever in this office—in person or by mail."

"Sell good merchandise at a reasonable profit, treat your customers like human beings, and they will always come back for more," Leon Leonwood Bean said.

Forget Advertising: Learn Customer-Driven Communication

All businesses are starting to feel like small town businesses when every one of their customers can talk to every other one. The biggest national brands are facing technology that lets customers thousands of miles apart act like they are in the same small town, exchanging their views on the brands' best and worst points. Companies that were used to controlling the message find that customers are paying more attention to friends' voices than corporate marketing. One bad customer experience can now touch thousands or millions of other customers.

Today, things are a lot like a small town, where all the customers know each other and share news and gossip about local companies. Small town business has adapted by treating customers like community. All businesses have a chance to adopt the small town strategies of treating customer service as though it's all you've got and using social tools to connect with customers. A number of big brands are pioneering treating customers as community in the online market.

The Change: Technology Allows All Customers to Easily Communicate with Each Other

Technology drives social change: social networks, social media, social sharing, and social games. Connected to the Internet and each other, consumers share what they think and how they feel every day. Eric Schmidt, former CEO of Google, estimated that every two days, people produce as much information as was created for all mankind for the 20,000 years leading up to 2003.

Peer-review sites like Urban Spoon, Yelp, and TripAdvisor mean that no business is immune to customer comments about their services, both good and bad. Anyone can pick up a cell phone or log in and have instant access to what other people think of any business, anywhere and anywhen. Suddenly, all businesses are forced to deal with a level of customer feedback and interaction that has escalated, sometimes into outright warfare.

It's not easy to restart an online reputation. Brian Clark, CEO of CopyBlogger Media, said, "You can't just move to a new town online."[1] The information available about every company online is forever.

Businesses of all sizes and from all areas face this same reality: Now that all customers can communicate with each other, it's like being in a small town. This is different from the previous decades, when company advertising could control "the conversation." Businesses could hire a famous pitchman or use a fancy slogan to tell consumers what to think and buy. Today, through reviews, the average consumer believes more of what peers say than what the company says.[2]

Impact on Brands

In 1999, the *Cluetrain Manifesto* set out 95 theses that addressed how to conduct business in a networked marketplace, where customers freely share information. The manifesto says, "Networked markets are beginning to self-organize faster than the companies that have traditionally served them. Thanks to the web, markets are becoming better informed, smarter, and more demanding of qualities missing from most business organizations."

The missing qualities that the *Cluetrain* mentions are the human qualities. Both markets and companies include human people, and they want to talk to each other in a natural, human way. "Markets are conversations." Thesis 12 states, "There are no secrets. The networked market knows more than companies do about their own products. And whether the news is good or bad, they tell everyone."[3]

For large companies, these ideas are not just radical; they are truly threatening. Companies were not built to work with this kind of communication. When Thesis 25 calls on companies to "come down from their Ivory Towers and talk to the people with whom they hope to create relationships," it is asking for major changes for most large companies and brands. The *Cluetrain* authors, Rick Levine, Christopher Locke, Doc Searls, and David Weinberger, recognize that "companies are deeply afraid of their markets."

In fact, all commerce on the web has gone social. Social-shopping tools help people share deals and recommendations with each other, to work together to achieve a better deal with group buying and share the same screen while they shop.[4] Retail sites now routinely include comments and reviews from customers. There are more layers of social interaction, including forums, list building, and connections to social networks. Shopping in front of a computer used to be a solo activity. Now it can be highly social and interactive.

It used to be that advertising could direct and control the conversation around a big brand's product or service. With social media, this is no longer true. While dissatisfied customers used to be able to complain to about seven people, with tools like Facebook, Twitter, YouTube, Google Plus, and LinkedIn, they can now tell 7 million people.

For example, when United Airlines broke Dave Carroll's guitar on a trip from Nova Scotia to Nebraska, he asked for compensation. When very little was forthcoming, Dave made a promise. Dave summarized it this way:

> In the spring of 2008, Sons of Maxwell were traveling to Nebraska for a one-week tour and my Taylor guitar was witnessed being thrown by United Airlines baggage handlers in Chicago. I discovered later that the $3,500 guitar was severely damaged. They didn't deny the experience occurred but for nine months, the various people I communicated with put the responsibility for dealing with the damage on everyone other than themselves and finally said they would do nothing to

compensate me for my loss. So, I promised the last person to finally say "no" to compensation (Ms. Irlweg) that I would write and produce three songs about my experience with United Airlines and make videos for each to be viewed online by anyone in the world.[5]

On YouTube, Dave's videos received more than 7 million views and reportedly affected United's stock price. United responded to the videos by offering Dave compensation, making a donation to a music school, and by saying it intended to change policies and use the video itself in customer-service training.[6] Competitor airlines viewed the video and changed policy to give special care in handling guitars.[7] Being part of a connected community now gives every single person a stronger voice, influencing many other consumers.

Consumers are more influenced by what their peers think about a product than how great a company claims it is. It is rare that a buyer does not check Amazon's peer-rating system before buying a product. Every buyer on eBay checks the reliability of the seller by looking at their reviews from other buyers. More and more consumers check Yelp before going to a restaurant or Tripadvisor.com before staying at a hotel.

Author Chris Colin believes that this "Yelpification of the Universe" is dangerous. He says the ratings, thumbs ups, and stars "eventually serve to curtail serendipity, adventure, and idiotic floundering."[8] There is a new opportunity for the big brands to regain some control through online reviews. If big brands can respond and shape what is being said about their companies, they can have increasing influence over their brand again.

Customer service can make or break brands. Although this is one of those "long-held truths," it's also supported by research like the American Express 2011 Global Customer Service Barometer. American consumers feel like most companies are failing to act as though customer service matters to their business. Nearly two-thirds of the surveyed consumers said they feel companies don't pay enough attention to customer service.

Although "surprise and delight" are common customer-service platitudes, few businesses accomplish them. Forty-two percent of consumers said that companies are basically helpful, but don't do anything extra to keep their business. Twenty-two percent said that they think companies take their business for granted.

The survey also confirmed that consumers no longer keep their opinions to themselves. They tell others about their customer-service experiences, both good and bad, with the bad news reaching a larger audience. Americans say they tell an average of 9 people about good experiences, and nearly twice as many (16 people) about poor ones. That multiplies the effect of every single customer transaction for brands, especially when shared over social media.[9]

In his new book, *We Are All Weird*, Seth Godin argues that the end of mass marketing has come and that the Internet makes it all possible, by being able to reach and affect a particular "tribe." Mass marketing can no longer push and mold the consumer into a universal "normal" just to sell more products. Seth states that marketing is far more efficient at reaching the weird. It's a lot easier to reach the "particular pocket of weird people with the stuff they are obsessed with."

In turn, it makes it easier to be obsessed, and marketers go along with it because they can reach a particular consumer. People can now easily congregate in tribes, so "weird is perversely becoming the new normal, at least in the small tribes...." As Seth reflects, "The community you choose mirrors you and further amplifies the unique interests you do have."[10]

Why Small Towns Already Work This Way

Small town business people deal with this every day and operate on treating all customers well. Everyone has always known everyone else's business. No one realizes that reputation is forever like small town people. No one knows about this kind of networked market like small town people.

A small town is the original model of this market. Small towns have a limited population that interacts more often, so information on reputation can spread much more quickly. One upset customer can walk into a coffee shop and spread the word of his experience with practically the entire town by afternoon. Happy customers can spread the word, too.

Business owners often see their customers downtown, in civic clubs, at churches, and at special events. Like Google today, reputation has always been forever in a small town. Small businesses in small towns have to live with this reality every single day.

Rural Regions Lead in Social-Media Adoption

The small town tendency to be social may explain why the Great Plains region is outpacing the East and West Coasts in social-media adoption by small and medium-sized businesses. Zoomerang, an online survey company, did a survey of more than 500 small and medium business decision makers. The regions with the highest percentage of these decision makers on social media were the Great Plains at 30 percent and the Southeast at 28 percent. The New England/NY region showed the lowest percentage of social-media adopters. Decision-makers for businesses in the Great Plains (22 percent) and Southeast (28 percent) are also among the most active via social media on behalf of their companies. Alex Terry, General Manager of Zoomerang, said:

> Less-populated areas or cities with a strong small business presence are relying more and more on cost-effective mass-communication tools for business news, customer support and acquisition, as well as networking. For people immersed in technology-driven cultures, such as Silicon Valley, this data may come as a surprise, but I believe they can learn from less technology-enriched regions.[11]

Social Media Is Like a Small Town, Everyone Says So

Experts in social-media marketing have begun using small towns as a way to explain the concept of networked markets to others. Seth Godin wrote about this idea as "island marketing." He stated that, "If your small business was based on an island, you couldn't afford to churn and burn through customers." Word will get around this small island about how you really treat your customers. With the technology of the Internet and social media, now every business is faced with this reality.[12]

Gary Vaynerchuk, author of *The Thank You Economy*, used the small town metaphor in a video called "Small Town Rules." Gary points out that we're all living by what he labeled as 1950s rules, and this will weed out many big brands that just don't care. As Gary says, when everyone knows everyone else, "you are playing by small town rules."[13] With social media, everyone now knows your business. This is what businesses and brands need to understand: that they need to care.

Social-business expert Liz Strauss explains how her dad's small town saloon in the 1950s created social networks much like the ones she creates online. "Truth is, what my dad did with his cash register, I do with my computer... the biggest difference is the speed and reach of the Internet. And I believe that entrepreneurial view is what gives every small biz an advantage in establishing a web presence using social-media tools."

"Every small town entrepreneur knows that no business thrives without being part of the community that we serve. Social-media tools simply stretch that community to give our business some visibility to the world."[14]

Benn Rosales at New Media Lab talks about small businesses creating their own small towns online:

> We talk a lot in the technology age about your online brand, or your online identity, but I submit that it's no longer just that— what it has become is your small town storefront brimming with small town folks that are active in the community minding your store. These folks are eager to help, share, and participate wherever they can, even with the local competitor to improve the lives of their local citizens.
>
> When boiled down in this manner, social media removes the need for large fan and friend followings; in fact it only solidifies the need for a handful of appreciative patrons to begin with. As you engage the community, your good name is spread by word of mouth within the community, creating a growing loyalty and following as the brand that stands behind their product and/or services. In other words, with only a handful of satisfied patrons, your growth is real and solid, rather than hollow and short-lived.[15]

Small town business people have learned to thrive on their own little islands, in places where their customers have long been communicating with each other. And the truth is, this was not limited to the 1950s. In small towns, it never went away. Small towns are still community-driven, people still spread news around like wildfire, and entrepreneurs still build businesses that succeed in a truly networked market. How do they do it? The great ones focus on their customers.

The Small Town Rule: Treat Customers Like Community

Smart small town businesses have been quick to transfer what they already know about how to treat customers to new tools that let them do it online. Smart businesses everywhere should pay attention to the online community building skills of small town businesses.

Treat Customer Service as Though It's All You've Got

Small town stores may be stereotyped as being friendlier and more help-ful than big retailers, but that isn't always true. It's something businesses have to cultivate and work hard to achieve consistently. The goal is to give customers a reason to choose that small town business over all those online competitors, those bigger businesses in the bigger towns, or the well-known national chains.

With the loss of geographic advantage, products and services are increas-ingly becoming commodities. Additionally, with a networked community where customers still talk directly to each other, customer service is the only sustainable competitive advantage for small business. "Customers are number one" has been a rallying cry within companies forever.

Companies often put this phrase in their mission statements. Ironically, few of them have been able to implement it. The level of service that most busi-nesses offer is pathetic, so that when a small business offers great service, it really sets them apart for the customer.

Mick Galuski is a small town business owner who understands the idea of completely customized personal service. He runs a comic and game store, Toy Soldier, in Amesbury, Massachusetts (population 16,000). New com-ics come in on Wednesdays. He could send out a generic message to all his followers on Twitter, saying, "New comics are in!" Instead, he'll send a direct message to his regular customers, like Chris Brogan. He sends Chris a photo of Chris's favorite comics, *his* weekly comics, the ones he knows Chris will rush in to get just as soon as he can.

"I wasn't that passionate about comics again until Mick MADE me more passionate, by keeping them top of mind for me every Wednesday," Chris said.[16]

Chris shared the story of another small town business that understands true personal service, *You Are Here Books*. It's located on a country road near Amesbury. The owner, Carolyn, not only special-ordered a book for him, she remembered him when he walked in a week later and offered him another book he might like. Chris said:

> That is the feeling I want from social media and how companies interact with it. It's this thing where people can spend a few extra moments to make a human connection instead of an "off the shelf" connection. I can buy from Amazon, and that's sometimes convenient, but I can't get the human touch of what I got with Carolyn.[17]

Use Social Tools to Connect with Customers

Combine the small town feeling of connecting with everyone and the new dynamics of business-customer relationships, and that equals social networks used for business. In the race to engage customers, some businesses have focused on collecting a certain number of followers or as many friends as possible. But, the raw size of the community may not be the most important point.

Small town entrepreneur Aliza Sherman said at the 140 Character Conference in 2009, "We are measuring small business success by big business standards. The right 15 followers may be much better than 1,500."[18]

If those 15 followers are engaged, interested, and sharing, that is better than 1,500 random followers with no interest in the business or 1,500 accounts that are now inactive.

United Linen is a restaurant-linen service based in Bartlesville, Oklahoma (population 35,000). Its Marketing Director Scott Townsend has actively experimented with social networks and other online tools to build and maintain customer connections. When the regular delivery schedule is changed, Scott communicates the new schedules through Twitter, YouTube, Facebook, and on the company website. That's in addition to the traditional technique of printing the schedule changes on customer receipts.

It's just one way to make practical use of these social networks. United Linen constantly makes videos that are helpful to customers, answer frequently asked questions, or demonstrate something useful. Because most of its customers are restaurants, it produced an entire series of videos on napkin folding. That helps the restaurants with training.

It also made a video showing how to refill the automatic paper towel dispensers it sells and services. Customers loved the video, seeing a demonstration of what they needed to know. It saved many phone calls and requests for help. Unfortunately, the big brand that makes the dispenser asked United Linen to take down that video, because it didn't like the way it made its dispenser look not-so-easy to use. United Linen has managed to maintain its small town sense of community and customer service even while using these new online tools to make the connections.

One small business that maintained its small town rules, even when it was engulfed by the ever-growing San Francisco Bay Area, is Tony & Alba's Pizza. The business kept that small town feeling as it interacted online. This is a conversation on Twitter between two friends talking about which pizza place to go to after practice:

> **schnaars**: @ryankuder speaking of which, are there any plans post practice?
>
> **ryanKuder**: @schnaars We're in. Should we head to Jake's for pizza?
>
> **tonyalba_pizza**: @ryankuder or Tony & Alba's maybe?
>
> **ryankuder**: @TonyAlba_Pizza Could you save us a table for 12 at Stephen's Creek so we don't have to wait?
>
> **tonyalba_pizza**: @ryankuder You got it what time? Do you want to pre order? I'll throw in fountain drinks.
>
> **tonyalba_pizza**: @ryankuder Just say that you are Ryan I'll have the table set in the TV room and I will send them a note. Just tweet like a bird-Just kidding

Tony & Alba's won a new customer by listening and following the small town rules. This can be done by small businesses, regardless of where they are located, to engage new customers.

No matter what tools a business uses, the customer has to be the #1 focus. The small town outlook still applies. Chapter 6, "How Big Brands and Small Businesses Are Thinking and Acting Small," goes into more detail about how to build community online and offline.

Applying the Small Town Rule to Big Brands

With the advent of social media, customer service is now the new market-ing. It has become the only sustainable competitive advantage and the cur-rent way to keep loyal customers. Advertising and company-directed public relations can no longer control the conversation about what people are say-ing about your company and products.

Large businesses have turned to social-media tools to monitor what is being said about them and get involved in that conversation. There are many well-known examples of companies that are good at this, such as Citibank, Intuit, Dell, Frito-Lay, and Maytag. Southwest Airlines also regularly moni-tors conversations on Facebook and Twitter about its companies and its competitors. Peachtree has provided a cool personality to its otherwise boring accounting software by engaging fans through social media.

A consumer can get better service from cable provider Comcast by tweeting @comcastcares than by calling its customer-service department. This was a huge turnaround for this cable company that was consistently blamed in public for its poor service. Comcast's former Director of Digital Care Frank Eliason says that, on his first day in his new job, he had to make a decision about how to respond to a website called www.comcastmustdie.com.[19] He decided that responding directly to customer concerns in a real-time man-ner would be the best way to defuse this type of hostility toward Comcast.

At the 140 Characters Conference in New York City in 2011, Becky and Cody Heitschmidt spoke about how L.L. Bean and Zappos were great examples of small town customer-service rules from large brands. Becky mentioned that L.L. Bean had never moved from Freeport, Maine, and never lost its small town customer service. Cody talked about how "Zappos epitomizes the small town customer-service model of caring deeply about every customer." Both brands were listening online and replied on Twitter. @LLBean thanked Becky for her kudos, and @Zappos_Service told Cody, "You just summed up our entire goal."

Tony Hsieh, CEO of Zappos, expanded on the small town touch, saying this:

> Ultimately, I think it comes down to the fact that people want to do business with people they feel connected to. And that's why most people, all other things being equal, if they're friendly with the neighborhood butcher, then they'd rather buy from him or

the guy that owns the convenience store down the street if he's your friend versus going to some big chain.

Now the problem is that usually the bigger chains offer lower prices and so on. So the small town merchant doesn't always win, but what people want is that personal, emotional connection to whomever they're doing business with. That's why we value the telephone so much, because it is personal.[20]

A personal online presence can create measurable business. Jon Swanson explains how that works from a customer's perspective. He was considering buying and using a domain name in a particular way. He had been following Network Solutions Social Media Swami Shashi Bellamkonda on Twitter for some time. So, when he saw Shashi at a conference, Jon asked him about what he wanted to do. Shashi was able to answer and recruit the customer, but it was entirely based on trust built online.

"Shashi isn't selling, he's conversing," Jon says. "You don't have to sell to bring benefits to your company from being online."[21]

Dell has taken social listening to a new height with its Social Media Listening Command Center. The company started this in an effort to stay connected to its customers worldwide through the conversations that were already happening about its products on the Internet. Dell is training its own people to embed community across the fabric of the company. It is also holding Customer Advisory Panel events where representatives listen to the good and bad from the customers' point of view. The customers said they had never experienced such an open dialogue with a global company before. In a display of transparency, Dell published the results on its Direct-2Dell blog, where everyone can see them.[22, 23]

Summary: All Customers Can Communicate with Each Other

Every business now deals with customers communicating directly with each other. The controlled marketing message has been replaced with individual conversations with customers. Review sites bring customer comments to everyone. Every brand is forced to do business in an environment much like a small town.

The Small Town Rule: Treat Customers Like Community

The corollaries:

1. **Treat customer service as though it's all you've got.**
   Product advantages come and go, but giving great customer service secures loyalty. Treat all customers as individuals, respecting their preferences as much as possible.

2. **Use social tools to connect with customers.** With social
   media, customer service has become the new marketing
   and the small business' only competitive advantage.

A Look Ahead

With more and more information and opinions being published every
day on the web, the world is becoming more diverse, but increasingly
connected. People are talking with people like themselves about every
company and their products.

Although the different platforms and tools used to share conversations online will change, there is little doubt that the habit of sharing
online is here permanently. Small town rules dictate that all businesses need to pay attention more to customer communication than
their own advertising message.

Powerhouse Small Town Brands

The Grasshopper Company
Moundridge, Kansas: Population 1,600

Grasshopper mowers have been used around the White House, in Red Square in Moscow, and at the Parc Monceau in Paris, but they all come from the same small town: Moundridge, Kansas.

The Grasshopper Company was founded by Elbert Guyer in 1969. Guyer drew ideas from his custom harvesting operation to come up with a better mower design, one that could turn in a very tight radius.

Moundridge is bypassed by Interstate 35, but this loss of geographic advantage hasn't stopped The Grasshopper Company from exporting its mowers to 40 countries. The company brings in foreign delegations several times a year, something that helps promote the entire region to international corporate customers.

More than 300 employees in Moundridge build mowers and equipment used to apply chemicals, aerate turf, remove snow, and clean up leaves and other debris. The first product to be exported was a portable grain dryer. Defying the stereotype of small town businesses as backwards or low-tech, The Grasshopper Company uses skilled manufacturing with computer-aided manufacturing and CNC (computer-controlled) machining.

People who buy Grasshopper mowers are treated as a community. Individuals are frequently featured in press releases from the company. A large section of the website collects and shares stories from people in different industries, customer stories are shared in a periodical called *The Hopper*, and the company maintains an active social network presence on Facebook and Twitter, sharing even more stories from its customers.

The Grasshopper Company is following the small town rules of locating anywhere despite geographic disadvantage and treating customers like community.

The Grasshopper Company is still family-owned and proudly says on its website, "No parent corporation or outside investors make the decisions at Grasshopper."

6

How Big Brands and Small Businesses Are Thinking and Acting Small

It is necessary now for every company to think and act small in business. Small town businesses are the model for achieving big goals while thinking and acting within the limits of small. Many areas of society are moving toward small and driving this change in business.

Brands face a credibility gap between big and small businesses in the minds of consumers. Small town businesses have an advantage in fitting what consumers want now. Big businesses are more comfortable speaking from the balcony, but small town businesses are best working in the crowd. Big businesses can learn some of these methods to better connect with customers.

As big brands work to build online communities, small towns offer lessons on how to build community effectively and how to deal with the negative side of small communities. Online tools offer new applications for small town methods of community building.

Unlike the go-go Internet bubble days in 1999, getting big fast is no longer the goal of smart companies. Keeping a business small is one way to keep the advantages of small. Learning to operate a big business like a small town business requires new methods and pays off with new benefits.

The Change: Society Is Cycling Back From Big to Small

Society is cycling away from everything that seems big, especially big companies and big retail. Small is definitely back. Today, people like small companies, small boutique hotels, small restaurants, small clubs, small groups of friends, and even small cars. Not too long ago, a small company had to appear big to get business. It is ironic that now many big companies want to appear small to show personal service and interaction with their customers.

Small may be the natural order of human organization. British anthropologist Robin Dunbar developed the theory of a social limit of 150 people for groups, the original scale of human interaction. From small villages, to small army units, to small work groups in companies today, 150 people is the limit of when it's possible for everyone in the group to know each other. Big business has long ignored this limit, but alternatives are now gaining attention. Small firms, small work groups, and small divisions join small businesses in optimizing for the right size and human scale.

Business and marketing author Seth Godin says, "Small is the New Big." He sings the praises of small companies, small churches, and small service providers. It's the personal contact, caring, and interaction that are possible in small organizations, which makes this an advantage. "Small means the founder is close to the decisions that matter and can make them, quickly," Godin said.

Small is not a limit on impact or on scope, just on size. Small firms can think big, and make a big difference, even without growing their ranks. Godin outlines how small has changed in business today. Small no longer means limited:

> Small means that you will outsource the boring, low-impact stuff like manufacturing and shipping and billing and packing to others, while you keep the power because you invent the remarkable and tell stories to people who want to hear them.[1]

Small businesses have created most of the jobs in the United States. Over the past 15 years, 64 percent of net new jobs came from small businesses, according to the Small Business Administration.[2] From 1999 to 2008, the large U.S. multinational corporations actually reduced their domestic employment by 1.9 million jobs, making them net job destroyers.[3]

Small is also rewriting what it means to network and connect with other people. Today, people in big cities are connecting across neighborhoods and networking with others outside of the old ways of connecting. With "meetups" and "tweetups," the old idea of a "power broker" has eroded. Why would someone wait for a power broker to make an introduction, when they can connect directly with the person they want to meet on LinkedIn?

Old-line civic organizations have slowly declined in most metropolitan areas. The total memberships of volunteer groups, like the Red Cross, Kiwanis, and Elks Lodge, have declined dramatically since the 1960s.[4] That statistic doesn't mean people don't care or don't want to be involved. Instead, it means that the ways of being involved in community are changing.

Online advocacy groups are on the rise, boosted by the array of communication tools that make it possible to organize and activate quickly. People organize action online through sites like Kiva for microlending, Idealist.org to match people and causes, and Change.org to build networks around issues.[5]

Impact on Brands

The reputation of big corporations has significantly fallen. People no longer trust a company just because it's big.

In its 2011 survey on customer service, American Express found that three-quarters of U.S. retail shoppers say smaller companies give them better customer service and that they have spent more money with those small companies because of it. More than 80 percent agree that smaller companies place a greater emphasis on customer service than large businesses.[6]

American shoppers believe in the importance of small businesses to their local communities. Overwhelmingly, people believe that small businesses make a positive contribution to their community and that they are a critical element of America's economy. When asked why they choose to shop local, a quarter of consumers talk about good, small town-style customer service, picking reasons like being greeted by name, being known, and receiving personal recommendations.[7]

In small businesses, immediate access to management is natural and expected. Online networks have made big businesses feel more like small businesses by providing a similar type of access. New communication tools have cut across corporate boundaries and given consumers access to CEOs and top executives. CEOs available on Twitter include Tony Hsieh of Zappos, skateboarder-turned-businessman Tony Hawk, Emilio Azcarraga of Grupo Televisa (the largest mass-media company in the Spanish-speaking world), Peter Gruber of Mandalay Entertainment, and Tony Fernandes of AirAsia. Thousands of other top executives are available on Twitter and other networks.[8]

Why Small Towns Create Community Interaction on a Human Scale

Small towns all share one key characteristic: They're small. This means fewer people, and that interaction still is mostly personal. Distances are smaller. "Across town" may mean just ten blocks. Businesses tend to be clustered, with more downtown retail districts than strip malls. The entire town may be considered within walking distance, which is the original human scale.

Networking is natural in a small town. With fewer competing networking events, all the local power players can get together more easily. The same few people are involved in most of the activities and projects.

A meeting over coffee or a chance discussion at the post office can change the course of a project, an entire business, or even the whole town. Small towns still have active civic, service, and professional groups. Although they are dwindling, there are still plenty of active small town clubs making a difference in a variety of ways.

In a small town, access to city government is easy. Everyone knows the mayor. Really knows them. The mayor of Alva, Arden Chaffee, was Becky's junior-high-school science teacher. Her mom has known him since they were both in grade school. It's not a big deal. The mayor before him, Stan Kline, ran the local body shop.

Anyone who wants to talk to the mayor can just do it. Anyone who wants to see the city manager can just show up at city hall. That level of access is impossible in big cities. The benefit is a chance to have a say in the community. City officials can't take all the advice everyone offers, but small town people have the chance to tell officials their opinions.

Small towns do business differently. Small town businesses fall into two stereotypes: the great and the awful. The great ones offer incredibly customized service, paying attention to what each customer wants. The awful ones set hours for their own convenience and have a "If you don't like it, tough!" attitude.

Great small town businesses maintain a personal link with customers. They pay attention to what each individual likes, and they try to cater to it. They will open up early or stay late just to help someone.

Why are small town businesses like this? Because few small town people had worked at big boxes, until Walmart came to town. Since then, the only retailers to survive were the ones giving outstanding customer service, selection, and remaining competitive on prices.

Businesses that grow up in small towns tend to still operate on a human scale. At United Linen in Bartlesville, CEO Mat Saddoris is sometimes answering phones over the noon hour, while everyone else goes to lunch. That kind of hands-on, personal involvement of top management is typical of small town businesses.

In a small town, it's common to have direct access to the owner or main manager of a business. Any customer can offer a compliment or complaint straight to the top. When the small business owners have to face their customers every day all over town, they learn how important customer communications really is.

The Small Town Rule: Be Proud to Be Small

Never before has there been a better time to be a small business. Customers trust small businesses more, customers think small businesses benefit the local economy more than big business, and small businesses can work better on a human scale. Building community on a human scale lets any business or brand connect with their customers in a more meaningful way, bringing the best of small to any business.

Build Community Through Involvement

In a fast-paced 24/7 transitory life, people are looking for more ways to be connected. This can be geographic or online. People build trust by being connected to each other. Because business is basically about people, successful involvement in a community is important.

Building community isn't about being on the balcony and broadcasting a message to a mass of listeners below. Building community is about getting out into the crowd, talking to individuals, and making connections. Maybe small towns have fewer balconies because small town people focus more on talking to each other than on broadcasting their message out into the air.

Getting involved in the community, organizations, and development activities is easier in a small town. When people show up, they can be involved and may even be asked to lead. This creates an advantage. By being involved in development organizations, small business people can influence the direction their small town is headed.

Smart business people use many different techniques to build community, no matter where they are based, geographically or online. Some of the techniques that build community within small towns are also applicable to the online community and offline community-building efforts by big brands.

Being friendly and responding to people comes naturally in small towns. For bigger-city businesses, adopting a friendly attitude can take some work. Being friendly and responding online is considered a best practice. Although it comes naturally to small town business people, it's a new idea for many people who are used to big cities or big corporations.

In online communities, replying or responding to messages builds a sense of community. When a Twitter follower says hello to a brand representative, the brand rep can say hello back. It's a small thing, but it is a building block of community. Offline, brands can respond to customers and fans in a friendly way, rather than an official and corporate way.

Knowing everyone's family in a small town is the result of living there for generations. Brands and businesses can adapt this by staying involved in their communities for the long term. Smart community builders come to stay. Although community building is a popular concept in business right now, short-term efforts that are abandoned quickly don't impress any customers. Effective brand efforts at community building involve a long-term commitment to be successful. This also applies to staying involved in online communities for the long term.

Approaching community by listening first and getting to know participants before any other steps contrasts with the short-term approach of hit-and-run product promotions. Smart business people plan for the long term, and that makes it easier to think about the long-term good of a community.

Eating together is a small town mainstay. Covered dish dinners, fund-raising meals, meals at churches, organizational banquets, and free feeds (where anyone who shows up is fed until the food runs out) give people a chance to sit down for a meal as a community. Brands and businesses can adapt this to include meals or virtual meals in their community-building efforts.

Although eating together doesn't seem practical for an online community, it can be adapted in several ways. Far-flung online communities can share virtual meals by video conference. Some social-media clubs meet virtually for breakfast. Open Coffee is a distributed event in the high-tech startup community. Open Coffee groups have been established in 80 cities around the world, but are tied together, building community around the idea of an online complement to the offline network around the startup community. Entrepreneur and London Open Coffee participant Phil Wilkinson says, "It's not even an event—it's a place where Internet people come and go for coffee, chat, and a cake."[9]

Businesses send packages of edible goodies to community members. Brands can share local food specialties, sending them as gifts to their community members. Twitter friends often virtually share food by offering, "Who wants coffee?" or sharing photos of delicious treats. It's just a way of being friendly and building community.

Being honest is a requirement in small towns. People actually do return found $20 bills or ATM cards stuck in bank machines. When Barry was speaking in Brookings, Oregon (population 6,300), he dropped some cash in the hotel lobby. The hotel manager went out of his way to find out who it belonged to and mailed the cash back to Barry. Brands and businesses that want to build an in-person community must be honest for the community's benefit. Honesty in an online community means resisting the temptation to shade the truth or hide behind the anonymity of the web.

Big businesses are more used to being able to control the message. If every message that comes out of the company has to be approved by legal, PR, and top executives, there is no room left for real, honest communication. The small town rule is to be honest and direct. Later in this chapter, the simple guidelines for online communication from Best Buy show that communication can be honest and direct without layers of approvals. Additional examples of corporate online communication guidelines are included in Appendix A, "Resources for Implementing the Small Town Rules."

Smart business people treat online communities like small towns and presume any dishonesty will be found out. "If you don't want your mother to read about it on the front page of the newspaper tomorrow, don't do it," is a small town maxim that applies just as much to brands today.

Watching out for each other is common in small towns. In local community-building efforts, people consider how their work will affect their neighbors. Watching out for each other online is similar: Consider how a project will affect online neighbors. Facebook has been criticized for failing to consider how changes in its service affect its millions of users and thousands of developers. Programmer Seth Call described working with the Facebook information interface as "one of the worst experiences as a developer I have ever had."[10]

Watching out for each other also means passing along opportunities to someone who is a better match. Online professionals frequently pass along notices of jobs, projects, and openings that others might be able to take advantage of. Big brands could also provide a service to their community by passing along opportunities and projects that are not directly related to the company, but do benefit their customers. The brand benefits when its customers benefit.

Small town people are helpful. If someone drops their packages on a downtown street, strangers will stop to help. If a car slides into a ditch in the snow, four farmers will offer to help pull it out. If an office burns down, two people may each offer free space until the business can find a new permanent location. (Yes, those are all true small town stories.)

For brands building online or offline communities, lending a hand can mean helping with others' projects, sharing information that others can use, or just answering questions. Especially in online communities, a helpful attitude leads to more sales than a selling attitude.

Small town people value their neighbors. Two neighboring farmers don't think of each other as competitors, but as peers. Those neighbors are the same ones who offer to help when it's needed. Local business people may be fierce competitors by day, but work on the same committee to build a new playground at the town park in the evening. It's not that all small town people like each other, but they share many of the same interests and most manage to work together as neighbors for the community.

In the online setting, the same rule about working together despite differences applies. In December 2011, a wide variety of businesses related to the WordPress online-publishing platform gathered for a conference called #MassiveCamp. The participants shared information with each other, even though most are competing in the same area. Their shared goal was to build a stronger system of healthy businesses that can support each other and the ecosystem of businesses around the WordPress platform.[11] Big brands can adapt this idea to create sharing spaces with their community and with other brands.

In another example of valuing competitive neighbors, a group of developers of small business web applications came together to create The Small Business Web. It's a loose trade association with the common goal of better integrating their many different and sometimes competing products. In 2010, group members handed out buttons that said, "Hug It Out," a play on the "slug it out" nature of most business competition.[12]

Getting involved is a small town way of life. Causes are more personal to small town people because the organizers know the people involved and the people who'll benefit. With fewer resources, small town people rely on each other to complete the projects the community needs.

Brands that stand back and wait for others to organize everything won't reap many benefits. People can see when a company is just jumping on to a popular cause or is late to the game. Some brands have never made an effort to get involved with causes. Cone Communications, a marketing firm that specializes in cause branding and corporate responsibility, says that 94 percent of consumers would switch brands based on their association with a good cause. The percentage has been increasing since Cone started monitoring the trend in 1993.[13] Brands can work together to get involved in causes. For examples, many major corporations support the nonprofit (RED), which helps eliminate AIDS worldwide. Gap donates 50 percent of all its profits from sales of (RED) logo products to this nonprofit.

Contributing means giving money, time, and facilities. In a small town, everyone has to help to make projects work, and support in name only is no support at all. Everyone from the mayor on down may be found picking up garbage on trash-off day.

For big brands and online communities, contributions are necessary to build community. A business that just slaps a banner ad on its website won't get as much benefit as a business that involves its people, shares its facilities, and donates its money. Bob Gilbreath, author of *Marketing with Meaning*, gave these guidelines for brands participating in cause marketing:

- **Do something brand-relevant.** Avoid jumping on popular but irrelevant causes.
- **Make sure it is meaningful.** Give enough to be significant.
- **Invest for the long haul.** Gilbreath said that Yoplait yogurt's Save Lids to Save Lives campaign has been successful for 11 years.
- **Create something that will engage employees.** That is an important part of building community from within.
- **Act quickly.** The Tide detergent Loads of Hope project immediately responds to disasters with trucks full of clothes washers and dryers.[14]

One of the biggest small town lifestyle benefits is the ability to let children have some freedom. Kids have a chance to play together spontaneously and make friends. Parents become friends, and business associates become friends, many times through the activities of their children.

Online community means adults get to do the same thing. All sorts of great things happen when people connect over play. Games like World of Warcraft online are new networking centers, the way the golf course was a generation ago. Brands can facilitate play and engagement among their community, online or off. Gamification, a trend of introducing game elements to other parts of business and life, has potential to address a wide range of problems. Imagine the potential of bringing a gamer's level of deep focus and concentration to the workplace or classroom and achieving an epic win over seemingly insurmountable problems.[15]

Large corporations use gaming extensively to build community. For example:

- SalesForce offers direct competition between users within an organization.
- Nike runners now have the ability to track and share challenges with their like-minded peers.
- By completing challenges in Microsoft's Ribbon Hero in Microsoft Office, users can compare skills with their friends.[16]

In a small town, people have more chance encounters. There are fewer choices of eateries and coffee shops, so people "run into each other" more often in small towns. Sometimes, it's possible to tell the time of day by which group of regulars is present at the coffee shop.

For brands, there are almost unlimited choices of places online and offline to build community, but it isn't wise to build in all of them. Smart community builders focus their efforts on fewer locations and practically become regulars, showing up at the same times to interact with many of the same people and to increase the chances of those chance encounters. Online, this can mean regularly participating in Twitter chats. Offline, brands can become regulars at industry events or put their people in situations where they can have more chance encounters. Former Apple CEO Steve Jobs had the headquarters building for Pixar Animation Studios designed to facilitate chance encounters and collaboration.

Downtown is often the center of the action in a small town. To be part of the community, small town people go downtown for concerts and events. Although many small towns have spread out over the decades, downtown still tends to be the cultural center.

For brands, the equivalent of going downtown is to be where the action is, at the center of the community. Online, isolated pockets of community exist on many different networks and sites, but probably aren't fertile ground for building a strong community for a business purpose. Rather than pouring effort into small communities, the small town rule is to find the center of action. In the section, "Move Past Connecting and On to Building Relationships," CRM tools help businesses find their own online downtown based on where their customers spend their time.

Small towns let practically anyone step up and lead. Anyone who shows up goes up. With fewer people to pick from, small organizations are happy to fill leadership roles and project chairs with new people. People have a chance to learn through successes and failures.

Brands building community can use this principle to get past the point of over-controlling and help build a sense of ownership in the community members. Turning over some leadership is a way of keeping the community fresh. Relinquishing control can be scary for businesses and brands, but the process itself is valuable. Successes and failures both help build a community, online or off.

"Communities are strongest when everyone plays a role," Boston University's Susan Fornier and Jump Associates' Lara Lee say in the *Harvard Business Review.* "Of and by the people, communities defy managerial control." One brand that let go of control without abdicating responsibility is skateboarding shoe brand Vans. It stays close enough to the community to know where it's headed, and then follows the community's lead, gathering product and design ideas from its members.[17]

What would small towns be without celebrations? Fourth of July parades are practically an icon of small towns. Woodward, Oklahoma, celebrates the Lesser Prairie Chicken Festival. Luling, Texas, holds an annual Watermelon Thump. Casselton, North Dakota, honors the Chokecherry with its own festival.

Brands can create celebrations, too. It strengthens the feeling of involvement to celebrate together. To celebrate the influencers in the small business space, smartphone maker Blackberry collaborated with two existing online publications with thriving communities, Small Business Trends published by Anita Campbell, and Small Biz Technology published by Ramon Ray. After nominations and voting, the 100 winning influencers were invited to a celebration together in New York City. The Blackberry brand benefitted from exposure to the existing online communities and celebrated the accomplishments of many small business influencers.

Network to Build Power and Accomplish Goals

Building community is all about giving a large group of people some common reference points and a shared culture. Within a community, there is another level of connection between individuals. Small town people are masters of networking, because it's necessary to their survival. In any small town, networks create economic and workforce development policy, connect influential individuals, conduct local government, and step up to lead community efforts. Brands and businesses everywhere can adapt these strategies to become influential in their local and online communities.

Local Networking

Networking with locals supports a sense of community, whether it's in a small town or a small online brand community. Fairview, Oklahoma (population 2,500), has a Chamber of Commerce networking lunch that is by far the best-rated benefit to members. Every leader in town attends regularly. Shattuck, Oklahoma (population 1,300), holds a Community Coffee that gets all the town's leaders in one meeting room. In a bigger town, those leaders are spread out between the chamber luncheon, the business-networking groups, the Rotary, business meetings, the Kiwanis, and the modern co-working get-togethers. It just isn't possible to have one event that draws all the potential players because there are too many of them.

Business leaders in urban areas can build their own local network. It can begin as simple as inviting another person out to lunch to talk about bringing together the key folks in the community. The next week, both participants can bring a friend. Existing networking frameworks, like the previously mentioned Open Coffee, can help provide structure. In online networking, the idea of a "local" networking can be stretched to include any group of regulars. Regular online networking events can take any form that works for the group. Entrepreneur and publisher Mike Sansone is pioneering a regular "local" networking event for small business people using Google Plus Hangouts.

It takes persistence, as there will be weeks when no one else comes. The ultimate result of making such a network is being at the center of the action. The person who convenes the network reaps a lot of benefits.

Step Up and Lead

Leaders can make things happen in a small town. In Becky's hometown of Alva, Don Benson was a longtime leader in the community. If there was a significant community project under consideration, he was probably behind it. He would put people together, call in some influence here, make a few phone calls there, and help make something happen. Every community has its Don Benson...or needs one.

Brands need their own people to step up and make things happen. In large companies, existing formal power structures can't provide the kind of leadership it takes to support a community. Business software firm SAP built an online community for its business customers, and it took one supportive member of the corporate board to overcome the internal opposition.

Today, the SAP Community Network has more than 2.5 million members and more than 3,000 posts per day.[18]

Economic Development

Getting involved in local economic development helps local business by improving the overall business climate. It also builds key networks and shows long-term support of the community. This is true in small towns, urban areas, and larger regions. Brands cannot expect an immediate payoff from this work, but have to think long term instead. Economic developers talk quite a bit about the benefits of growing clusters of related businesses together, including a more experienced workforce, specialized suppliers, shared distribution, and specialized education.[19]

Each small town or urban neighborhood has its own arrangement for economic development. Some town governments employ an economic developer, while others have separate boards or a county organization. Many urban areas have connected with their outlying rural areas to form large economic development regions. Outside organizations also get involved in economic development, including universities, technical centers, and chambers of commerce. The quality of work these groups do largely depends on the quality of the people involved. Economic development can be the center of messy local politics, so it calls for a little observation and research before getting involved.

Workforce Development

Another segment of economic development to consider is the workforce development board. Whether urban or rural, every region has one, and its goal is to produce a better qualified workforce to meet businesses' needs. These boards bring together people from education, representatives from businesses, and many government groups that have some relationship to jobs for people, including human services, unemployment or employment offices, and vocational rehabilitation.

Workforce boards usually need business representatives from a wide variety of industries. This is one place brands and businesses can influence their future supply of qualified workers. Lots of prominent economic development professionals believe that the education system from early childhood through post-secondary influences the local economy. The Montana

Associated Technology Roundtables even affirmed that at the top of every page of its website: "The State with the Best Education Wins!"[20]

Government

In a small town, getting elected or appointed in the local government is less difficult than in a major city, like Chicago. Each small town has a city council or town board and a lot of committees, boards, councils, work groups, and task forces. With a limited group of people to choose from and many slots to fill, small town business people who show up and participate are more likely to find themselves appointed to something or be able to stand for election themselves.

In a bigger city, the government involvement usually only happens for the wealthy (who have the time), the professional volunteer (who has the money or doesn't want the money), and the politically motivated (who need the government to do something for their business). Brands can become involved in local government if they focus on one part of the geographic community or one vertical segment. Local neighborhoods may have their own local government or governance functions that are more open to involvement.

Other Community Groups

Many small towns have a wide variety of groups, like the Rotary, Kiwanis, Jaycees, Ambucs, General Federation of Women's Clubs, Home and Community Education, or fraternal organizations, like the Elks, Oddfellows, and the Moose. Those are ready-built networks to tap into. Business people can pick one where they like the projects or already know some members.

In bigger cities, there are many organizations, both old and new. The key is to actually get involved, because people who help community groups accomplish their goals become valued in those networks. That can benefit brands in their own efforts and develop local support for the brands.

Churches are central to community in many small towns. In some areas, the churches are built at the geographic center of town. Usually, small towns center on church life more than big cities. More rural people than urban people attend church regularly, and those who do are more active in church activities. Churches also play a key role in social services and charity. In some small towns, the church you attend can influence your social status. Churches are definitely centers of networking.

Some brands choose to support religious causes that are closely associated with their brand. Faith-based marketing has become one of many segments within cause marketing, although it is still not mainstream. Israeli wine marketer Premier Wine Imports is pairing wines with Jewish nonprofit organizations, donating 10 percent of every sale.[21]

Go Online

Social networks and online communications can connect business people with industry peers worldwide. By using LinkedIn, Facebook, Twitter, blogs, and other tools, small town people have the opportunity to expand their network beyond the local. Shannon Ehlers lived and worked in tiny Soldier, Iowa (population approximately 300). When he was working as a Traditional Chinese Medicine chemist, he didn't have a lot of industry peers anywhere near him. But, he was a master of using LinkedIn to connect, and not just within chemistry circles. Shannon asked and answered lots of business questions on LinkedIn, connecting him with peers all over. Any brand or business can effectively use this same technique, whether based in a rural or urban area.

All kinds of affinity groups now connect on Twitter at regular times for tweet chats. Using a pound sign (#) at the beginning of the chat name makes it easy for users to search Twitter for the messages on that topic in the sea of tweets. People who blog connect at #BlogChat. Customer service is the topic at the #Custserv chat. Farmers and ranchers gather at #AgChat. Tourism professionals share tips on #TourismChat. It's another way of networking outside of geographic boundaries. More information on Twitter chats is included in Appendix A, "Resources for Implementing the Small Town Rules."

The Antidote for the Negatives

It's no secret that there are downsides to small towns and networks. The stereotype is that, in a small town, everyone knows everyone else's business—sometimes even before they do! It's a stereotype because it has some truth. Most small towns do have a gossip about every 20 feet, and most online brand communities have gossips, too. Here are some of those negatives and what brands and businesses can learn from them:

Everyone knows everyone else's business. It's true, but only up to a point. Becky doesn't know everyone in her hometown of Alva, OK (population

4,900), but she knows quite a few. She doesn't participate in the local gossip, and she jokes that she's the last to know about all the news. Most people in Alva have never heard of her.

For businesses and brands building an online community, it's important to remember that there are benefits to having people talk about them, even when it's news they would rather have kept quiet. In today's transparent world, it's tough to keep a secret forever. In fact, there is another benefit of this kind of community knowledge, where everyone knows everything, because it builds strong ties in communities.

With the same few people involved in everything, a small town can be too much of a closed system. Small town Economic Development Expert Jack Schultz called this the STP: the Same Ten People. (If a town is small enough, make that the same three people.)

The lesson for any brand is to make an effort to mix up teams and stay away from the STP mentality. Tiny online communities will struggle. As online communities grow, additional staff will be needed to maintain them.

Small town folks resist and dismiss outsiders and outside ideas. It is also called NIH (Not Invented Here). Anyone who didn't grow up here, or whose family hasn't been here for generations, is dismissed. Those fancy big-city ideas are doomed because "we tried that once." The small town locals would never even consider them.

Brands and businesses don't have to be the know-it-all. Community-building efforts benefit from openness to ideas, even ones that seem foreign.

It's true that a lot of small towns resist change. This is the way things have always been, and it leads to generational conflicts. "We're waiting for them to die off," really does get said. (Oh, wait, Becky has even said it. Don't tell anyone, OK?) Sometimes, successful efforts just have to go around those roadblock people. This may mean duplicating their efforts or creating something new or related.

Probably every person who has worked for a big business can see the parallel; resistance to change is built into most large companies. Brands can use the same techniques as small town people: Go around those roadblock people or wait for them to retire.

Beware the CAVE people. This is another Jack Schultz acronym. It means Citizens Against Virtually Everything, and small towns know this well. Remember, if no one hates it, it may not be anything important. Negativity and politics feed on themselves. Those CAVE people head to the coffee shop early, and they try to stir up as much trouble as they can in the morning. Then, they have a busy afternoon trying more of the same. Even well-justified concerns can get magnified out of proportion.

This happens in the online world, too. Firestorms can hit any company, as one person launches into a tirade and gathers supporters. It can be based on a real problem or just an out-of-control rant. What can brands and businesses do? Here are a few tried and true suggestions:

- **To avoid a firestorm in the first place, overcommunicate.** Although it's easier to get the word out to everyone in a small town, it still takes multiple repetitions and multiple channels. Online, the same rules apply: Repeat the message and use as many media channels as reasonably possible.

- **Don't ignore a firestorm.** Ignoring an individual who is ranting for no reason is OK, but ignoring a problem is asking for a bigger problem. Online, the irrational flamers can be ignored by brands, but underlying problems that are ignored just grow.

- **When approaching a firestorm online or in person, it pays to remain above it.** Inform, but don't argue. Don't get down to their level. Pigs love to get into the mud, because that is where they are comfortable. Don't go there. Smart small town leaders, and smart business leaders, will address answers to the entire community, not the individuals in a lynch mob or online firestorm.

- **Keep the focus on the community needs.** Don't get distracted into focusing on the complainers, the side issues, or the past. Online, brands must focus on needs of the community itself, rather than any other issues that get brought into the discussion.

- **Always thank people for engaging.** Successful small town leaders try to be polite, even to those who act rude. For brands, thanking people for feedback is crucial. Acknowledging that customers have a point of view that is being listened to is important.

- **Acknowledge the truths.** Many rants are tied to at least a seed of truth, online and offline. Being honest about those points is easier than trying to rationalize or cover them. For brands, it can be difficult to get permission from the layers of bureaucracy to acknowledge an error, but when it can be done, it builds trust.

- **Fix what can be fixed.** Nothing sucks the life out of a small town firestorm faster than solving the underlying problem. For brands, making corrections or changes may take more time, so it helps to keep community members informed during the process.

- **Use small town coffee-shop skills.** When small town people walk into the hometown coffee shop, they know that different situations and different people call for different approaches. Sometimes, they have to sit down and engage the complainers in conversation. Sometimes, a laugh is the best response. Online community managers will need to perfect a similar set of skills in reading people and situations.

- **Know when to move on.** This is another coffee-shop skill. Sometimes, the best thing to do is not engage them at all or end a conversation. Don't be afraid to do the same online.

- **When it gets worse than anyone can imagine, call in some outside facilitators.** Small towns can invite in a neutral party that has credibility who can ask the questions that no one else can admit need to be asked. Online, the neutral party might be a respected online person, or even a mediator in an online community.

Move Past Connecting and On to Building Relationships

In a small town, business owners know which real life social networks their customers belong to. They can keep track of which people attend which church, who belongs to the Rotary Club or the Chamber of Commerce. By being active in these local networks, small town people naturally build broader relationships with customers outside of business.

Knowing each customer as a real person is a strength of the best small town businesses. New tools allow any business to keep that kind of small town connection even as their business grows or moves online. Many small businesses keep an email address list of customers but fail to make much use of it.

In fact, most small businesses don't do very well at recognizing and connecting with new customers or new prospects who email them. Customer Relationship Management (CRM) tools can change that. CRM tools range from simple address books that let businesses keep track of contacts to complex relationship tools with databases, calendars, and more, in one system. Some, like BatchBook, are well-suited for small business, and some, like SalesForce, are designed for big brands.

It is important to systematically stay in contact with prospects, connectors, and influencers, even when there is not an obvious opportunity. Remember, a business can't sell anything to anyone; it just needs to be there when people are ready to buy. If businesses keep customer relationships current, they will be top of mind when the customers have a need. Using CRM can help any business accomplish several important goals:

- **Treat people like more than just an email address.** Small businesses want to get to know customers—their likes and dislikes. CRM tools can help businesses learn more about individual customers even when they only connect online. That extra information about customers can help a business build better relationships, just like a small town business.

- **Build stronger connections across networks.** There are some people that it pays to get to know better and connect with in more than one way. Examples include a business' biggest supporters, colleagues at other businesses, suppliers, network members, or elected officials. Businesses can use CRM tools to see when these influential people are active on a social site they also use and connect with them individually. It's just like small towns. When a business person finds out that a friendly acquaintance from church is also a member of the same professional club, they naturally want to connect. In fact, people often recruit their good friends to join projects that they support, because they know they can work well together.

- **Know where customers hang out online.** By looking at which sites customers use most, businesses can decide where to focus their online efforts. If the customers aren't on Twitter, but they are all over Flickr, the business should use that to decide where to focus. Using CRM tools in this way can help focus time and effort where it will create the most results. Go where the conversation is.

- **Focus attention on the right people.** Most of these services give businesses and brands an idea of who is more influential among their contacts. This allows them to invest limited time and attention carefully. Clearly, this is not an excuse to treat anyone poorly. It is a tool to help people make decisions. There has been a lot of online discussion and debate about influence and measures of relative importance like Klout, Kred, and PeerIndex scores. Undoubtedly, new systems will be developed. No matter how it's measured, smart businesses will treat all people well, but will also recognize that some people are worth bending over backward for. It's really not that different than the small town business, where the person behind the counter knows every customer individually and can instantly recognize the more influential customers.

- **Growth means every small business will need tools like this.** As a business grows and starts to connect with more and more people, the staff members are less able to keep all those details in their heads all the time. Top-level politicians have a personal aide who whispers names and details to them at just the right time. Who is just married, and who is now at a new company? Until small businesses can afford the personal staff to follow them around, they can use some online equivalents in social CRM.

Build Community Among Customers

There is now a place beyond great customer service that can bind the loyalty of customers even more closely to a business than having great products or providing a great service. That place is called community. The mission or purpose of most companies inevitably talk about providing a great product and excellent customer service. For example, Domino's Pizza's mission is *"Exceptional People On A Mission To Be The Best Pizza Delivery Company In The World."* This is part of Domino's "Vision and Guiding Principles," including these not-exactly-earth-shattering statements:

- "We Demand Integrity.
- Our People Come First.
- We Take Great Care Of Our Customers.

- We Make Perfect 10 Pizzas Every Day.
- We Operate With Smart Hustle and Positive Energy."

However, the starting point for every small business owner is to have a great product, people, and service. Stating this in a mission statement is not a competitive advantage and, to be successful today, the small business owner needs to go much further. He needs to form a community with his customers.

Nick Sarillo has been running his pizza restaurants, Nick's Pizza and Pub, in the suburbs of Chicago for more than 15 years. When Nick started, he wanted to have a purpose to his small business beyond offering a great product with great service. So, he created "Pizza on Purpose."

The mission statement that Nick came up with 15 years ago for his restaurants was *"Our Dedicated Family Provides This Community an Unforgettable Place to Connect with Your Family and Friends, to Have Fun and to Feel at Home."* Notice that this mission statement does not talk about having great food or friendly people to serve the customer. Nick set out to use his restaurants to create a community where people can connect.

Isn't this the goal that most businesses have for social-media business efforts and that most small towns have for building community? His restaurants now support more than 40 organizations in his community through fundraisers.

Nick's small business gives something beyond great customer service. He offers a community for his customers and a way for them to connect with each other. When they are at Nick's, they feel good about themselves, their community, and his business.

As a result, there is no longer a dividing line between his company and his customers. With his business, Nick created a community that just happens to be a pizza restaurant. This is similar to Zappos, where it's not a company that just sells shoes, but a company that delivers great service, regardless of its product.

There is no better way to create more loyal fans than for them to be part of a community and have them raving about a business. Forget creative marketing. Forget great customer service. Go to the place called community and a business will have its most sustainable competitive advantage: the raving loyalty of its customers.

Keep the Business Small

Business author John Warrilow has argued that smaller is actually better when building a business. While most entrepreneurs are pushed to create $200 million businesses, he says it's better to build a $2 million business. He listed six advantages: Founders can do what they love, they can keep all of the equity, they only need ten wonderful team members, they can become rich enough and have the choice to live where they want, and they can still have a life.[22] These are advantages that reflect the principles of small town business.

Jason Fried and David Heinemeier Hansson are the founders of 37 Signals, an online collaboration service. Together, they wrote an entire book, *Rework*, about how they bucked the traditional wisdom about successful business. Further bucking the traditional system, the book was initially self-published. They dedicate one full chapter to the question, "Why Grow?"

> Small is not just a stepping-stone. Small is a great destination in itself. Have you ever noticed that while small businesses wish they were bigger, big businesses dream about being more agile and flexible? And remember, once you get big, it's really hard to shrink without firing people, damaging morale, and changing the entire way you do business.[23]

Small business can still mean big revenue. Hopunion LLC forms the hops supply chain for craft-beer production, and its use of FedEx distribution to overcome geographic disadvantage is featured in Chapter 4, "Adapting to the 'Anywhere, Anywhen' Business World." It chooses not to supply the two mega-brands: Anheuser-Busch InBev and MillerCoors. Instead, it focuses on craft brewers. These are local brewers, independently owned, that produce less than 6 million barrels of beer annually. As a group, craft brewers are growing fast. In 1978, there were only 42 breweries in the United States. Craft brewers now number 1,700 in the U.S. and are managing to increase their revenue 12 percent, even though the overall volume of beer consumption in America has dropped slightly. That growth has helped Hopunion grow from $2 million in revenue in 2002 to $40 million in 2010. With fewer than 50 full-time employees, Hopunion is a small business that has built big impact and big revenue. Hopunion head Don Bryant says:

The nice thing is, now craft's driving the bus. Historically, it was all A.B.; it was all the big guys. So we're having a little bit of fun now having some leverage.[24]

Apply the Small Town Rule to Big Brands

Years ago, small companies wanted to appear big. This happened through typed communication on company letterhead, with printed envelopes that had been through a postage machine. In one of Barry's startup businesses, he used to hire friends when customers came to town to make his company appear bigger. He even went as far as to have the computers dial the telephone so the company appeared busier. The proliferation of computers, printers, and electronic communication allows businesses of all sizes to look big. By looking at a website, it is difficult to tell how large a company is.

In fact, small businesses now have an advantage with small town rules. Because consumers want to be treated like an individual, something they are more likely to get at a small company than a large corporation, big companies are now trying to appear small through customizing and personalizing products and services. Customizing and personalizing are two ways of acting small for big business.

Technology has allowed personal interaction for most electronic buying and service situations. When a customer logs on to buy something from Amazon, the site calls the consumer by name (if the web browser's "cookies" are enabled) and can tell her what she bought in the past and what she might like to buy in the future. Unfortunately, no such "faux personalization" is available when a shopper enters a big-brand retail store.

Ever since Burger King promised in 1974 that customers could "Have it Your Way" (customize your burger), big brands have tried to customize everything. The promise of customization made a comeback, as the campaign was revived in 2004.[25] Small town rules dictate that large corporations now want to appear small.

In recent years, this power of one has been served up by many companies. Keurig Coffee's K-Cup machines are designed to quickly brew a single cup of coffee or tea. The company claims that its products brew 2.5 million beverages a day (or 6 percent of all the coffee made daily).[26]

Ford Motor Company has an online design program that allows customers and browsers to design their own Mustang. Coca-Cola's new retail beverage dispenser can generate 100 different kinds of sparking and still beverages. Nike has allowed consumers to design their own shoes for many years.

Recently, Kraft introduced MiO liquid flavor enhancer. It allows customers to put as much or as little as they like of one of six flavors in their water. The company's advertising tag line is, "Make it Yours! Like Control? How Refreshing!" Even Ore-Ida's steam-and-mash potato product tells customers to "Steam in the microwave, then mash your way!"

When it's not possible to keep the entire business small, one solution is to keep work units small. Two large brands that have built a sizeable success while staying with small work units are Gore and SRC.

W.L. Gore & Associates is known to almost everyone in the U.S. from its Gore-Tex clothing. It's also known for appearing on "top places to work" lists year after year. There are no organizational charts. Every person who works at Gore is an associate. That is the only job title.[27] Working groups and even manufacturing plants are limited to 150 people, even though the total number of associates company-wide now exceeds 8,000.[28]

SRC (Springfield Remanufacturing Company), from Springfield, Missouri, (population 159,000) received national attention in the 1980s when it used the Great Game of Business to teach every worker to read and understand financial statements. Because every worker is also an owner of the business, each one knows how to keep score and has a stake in the game. Over the last 20 years, the company has added almost 60 related companies, with almost 1,200 total employees. One key to SRC's success is maintaining small work units.

CEO Jack Stack said, "It's very, very hard to get passion in the organization over 250, over 400 people. You lose the touch that you really need in terms of building the teamwork that you want."

To keep the numbers small, SRC creates separate new divisions in new firms. The efforts spent to educate every worker on the basics of business paid off. SRC workers know how to run a business. When a worker creates a new opportunity, SRC knows the workers can handle it as a nearly independent business.[29]

The small town rules also make it important for big brands to relate to customers on a personal and individual level. One way to do that is to have evangelists out in the community promoting the merits of a company. This can be done effectively by paid corporate employees (Apple has official evangelists, including Guy Kawasaki, earlier in his career), but it is done mostly by mobilizing the company fans through social media. This means getting many of the company employees involved in the social-media effort and not just the assigned customer service or social-media department.

For example, Best Buy assigns only 13 "community connectors" for 6 million customers. However, it also empowers all of its employees to participate, and 3,000 of them are involved. The guidelines that Best Buy gives these employees are key to its success.

The guidelines tell employees what they should do:

1. **Disclose your affiliation.** If you talk about work-related matters that are within your area of job responsibility, you must disclose your affiliation with Best Buy.

2. **State that it's your opinion.** When commenting on the business, unless authorized to speak on behalf of Best Buy, you must state that the views expressed are your own. Hourly employees should not speak on behalf of Best Buy when they are off the clock.

3. **Act responsibly and ethically.** When participating in online communities, do not misrepresent yourself. If you are not a vice president, don't say you are.

4. **Honor our differences.** Live the values. Best Buy will not tolerate discrimination (including age, sex, race, color, creed, religion, ethnicity, sexual orientation, gender identity, national origin, citizenship, disability, or marital status or any other legally recognized protected basis under federal, state, or local laws, regulations, or ordinances).

The guidelines also spell out what employees should *not* talk about:

1. **The numbers.** Nonpublic financial or operational information. This includes strategies, forecasts, and most anything with a dollar-figure attached to it. If it's not already public information, it's not your job to make it so.

2. **Promotions.** Internal communication regarding drive times, promotional activities, or inventory allocations, including advance ads, drive-time playbooks, holiday strategies, and Retail Insider editions.

3. **Anything that belongs to someone else.** Let them post their own stuff; you stick to posting your own creations. This includes illegal music sharing, copyrighted publications, and all logos or other images that are trademarked by Best Buy.

4. **Confidential information.** Do not publish, post, or release information that is considered confidential or top secret.[30]

Another technique for a big brand to think small is to publicly support small business. One brand making a big move into small business is American Express, with Small Business Saturday. Because the focus of Black Friday retail shopping has been on major brands and chains offering deep discounts, AmEx developed Small Business Saturday in 2010 to promote spending the next day at small, independently owned retail businesses.

More than 100,000 small businesses participated and saw measurable increases in sales. In 2011, Google, Facebook, and Twitter joined the effort with advertising credits for small business to promote their participation. FedEx and other promotional partners got on board, along with hundreds of shop local advocacy groups.

AmEx has a vested interest in small businesses, as independent merchants have a choice whether or not they accept American Express cards. AmEx also maintains OPENForum.com, a place where business owners can connect with each other and learn from small business experts.

For similar reasons, Visa has developed the Visa Business Network. It also includes educational content and chances for businesses to connect with each other, as well as a goal-oriented section where business can declare and then work toward a goal for the business, such as "promote my business on Facebook" or "set up an accounting system."

Summary: Society Is Cycling Away from Big to Small

Small is no longer an insult. Small can be beautiful. In a world where customers prefer small, it makes perfect sense to look at how small town businesses have succeeded at being small.

The Small Town Rule: Be Proud of Being Small

The corollaries:

1. **Build community through involvement.** Come down from the balcony and join the crowd. Let go of the idea of broadcasting one message to a uniform audience. Start making connections with people as individuals to build community. That starts with being friendly, building for the long term, sharing meals, being honest, watching out for others, being helpful, valuing neighbors, getting involved, playing together, having chance encounters, letting others step up and lead, and celebrating together.

2. **Network to build power and accomplish goals.** Beyond building networks of customers, businesses and brands have the opportunity to build a stronger community through local networking, leadership, economic development, workforce development, government, and community groups. Besides local efforts, businesses and brands can take these projects online.

3. **The antidote for the negatives.** Each small community comes with downsides. The answer to most is better communication and openness.

4. **Move past connecting to build relationships.** Customer-relationship management is more than a category of software, it's a way of doing business following the small town rules. Treat people as more than just an email address, build stronger connections, connect in multiple ways, focus attention on the right people, and use the right tools to maintain this as the business grows.

5. **Build community within your customers.** Businesses and
    brands now have an opportunity to extend the same
    methods of building community to their customers.

6. **Keep your business small. Small can be the right size
    for a business.** Not every business is destined to be the
    next multinational, and that should not be the only goal.
    Thinking and acting small can mean staying a small busi-
    ness, keeping small work units within a larger company,
    making interactions personal, or showing support for small
    businesses.

A Look Ahead

As connectivity increases, the world is actually breaking down into
small identifiable pieces. More personal and fewer mass marketing
conversations are happening between companies and their customers.

Preference for small over large is part of the huge pendulum swing
that is changing America right now. The swing over to large mass
markets took decades, and the swing back to small will likely last quite
a while. The cycle will go back eventually, but don't expect it to happen soon.

Powerhouse Small Town Brands

Longaberger Baskets
Dresden, Ohio: Population 1,529

Handmade, signed, and dated Longaberger baskets are a mainstay of country and casual decorating, and the Longaberger Company has grown far beyond baskets.

The basket-making in the Longaberger family started when J.W. Longaberger apprenticed with the Dresden Basket Factory in 1919. At the time, baskets were part of the industrial and manufacturing base of Ohio, used in local pottery factories and homes. Eventually, baskets were replaced with bags and boxes for everyday use.

J.W.'s son Dave had an entrepreneurial spirit. Always earning money at something, his family called him the "25-cent millionaire." He worked a variety of jobs and operated several local businesses, overcoming personal obstacles and disadvantages.

In the 1970s, Dave noticed that baskets were coming back into fashion. He founded The Longaberger Company and soon expanded into an old mill building where his mother had once worked. It remains a family-owned business, with Dave's daughters, Tami and Rachel Longaberger, as the current owners.

The Longaberger Company has grown to the point that *Forbes* lists it as one of the country's 500 largest private firms, and it is still based in the Dresden area. Headquarters are in the nearby town of Newark, Ohio (population 47,000).

Today, the company also sells pottery, other decorative items, and specialty foods. Some 45,000 independent consultants sell Longaberger products through home shows directly to consumers. Longaberger destinations reflect the national interest in the local culture and include eight factory stores, a golf club, a hotel, and the Longaberger Homestead. The homestead is a combination of attractions with local flavor, including a factory store, Dave's old workshop, a vault of limited quantity baskets, hands-on basket-making activities, tours, meeting space, events, and vacation packages. Guests who make purchases on site at a Longaberger destination can give credit for the sale to their local independent consultant, supporting the home-based direct sales force.

"People appreciate personal service and high quality," Dave said.

The Longaberger Company is following the small town rules of being local and treating customers as community.

7

Going Local, Even When You Are Big

The renewed interest in all things local presents a challenge to national brands and big businesses. A major shift in consumer thinking has customers paying attention to the potential local economic impact of their purchases.

As brands and businesses start to come to grips with this change, small town businesses already have. Small towns define the essence of local. While the common image of small towns is that they are part of the past, small towns did not disappear after the 1950s. They are the model of the characteristics that make a community, even an urban community, a desirable place to live.

Brands and businesses can begin by connecting with a local culture and place, and then build engagement with customers through local stories. Shop local campaigns provide clues to businesses wanting to build their local economy and to brands wanting to connect with the local movement. Brands can "go local" without losing their national identity.

The Societal Change: The Local Movement Is Here

The seemingly separate trends of shopping at local businesses, eating local foods, and traveling to local attractions have all rolled up into a complete movement affecting all of society.

In one example, local foods dominate national food trends, taking 5 out of the top 20 spots in a 2012 National Restaurant Association survey of chefs. Those five local food trends were locally grown produce, local meats and seafood, hyperlocal items, farm-branded ingredients, and local beer and wine.[1] That kind of local focus is taking root in every aspect of society. Consumers are far more interested in where their money is going and what potential impact their purchases may have. People are paying more attention to where products are manufactured. "Made in USA" is again an important label, but made in the local state is even better. Made in China is sometimes a black mark on a product, even though plenty of Chinese-made goods are still selling. Fair-trade goods sell for higher prices and can sell better than their regular counterparts.[2]

The Hartman Group's Pulse Report on Consumer Understanding of Buying Local tried to sort out what people think of as "local products." It turns out that "local" means a lot of things. Half of the people surveyed agree that products made within 100 miles are local. A third would agree that "local" is anything made within their state. Only 4 percent would agree that anything from within the region, like New England or the Midwest, was local, and 4 percent also think broadly enough to consider anything made in the U.S. as a possible definition of buying local.[3]

Beyond considering where products are made, consumers are increasingly paying attention to supporting small local businesses. On a neighborhood scale, Stacy Mitchell with the New Rules Project laid out a manifesto for the new local economy movement in 2009. She pointed to the growing popularity of local food through new farmers' markets, food co-ops, and neighborhood greengrocers. Local retail also has seen new life, with new independent bookstores, hardware stores, and record stores. More than 130 cities have formed local business alliances, with some 30,000 businesses as members.[4] "Cash mobs" are using social media to organize customers to support local businesses in groups. Now that shop local campaigns are everywhere, a simple "Shop Local" slogan is no longer enough to sway consumers. More savvy consumers are becoming wary of "local washing" (claiming a product is local with only a bare minimum of localness) and are not automatically accepting all products labeled as local.

Small retailers have noticed that shop-local awareness is increasing among their customers. In 2011, American Express OPEN's Retail Economic Pulse surveyed 600 retail small business owners with storefront locations. Most of them (51 percent) believed the buy-local sentiment is growing, and 55 percent believed that it helps small businesses compete.[5]

Impact on Brands

Brands have to navigate this shifting maze of consumer and business preferences. National brands are still powerhouses of the economy, but consumers are increasingly asking for local alternatives. Whole Foods has built a business model on local foods. It even has its employees wear shirts that say, "Local is the New Black." Groupon solicits deals from local merchants across the country and offers them back to local consumers. Dex One focuses on helping consumers find local small businesses when they are ready to purchase. Its "yellow pages" directory and now DexKnows online search have long connected the local consumer with the local business.

Manufacturing businesses are more worried about local connections, too. American companies are learning that a longer supply chain means more opportunity for problems. Although there is no escaping the connectedness of our global economy, there is a move to buy materials more locally to ensure a more reliable supply. *Newsweek* highlights the tight credit markets and political protectionism that are accelerating this trend. Governments around the world have passed new trade tariffs and offered subsidies to exporters and stimulus funds to products produced locally. This is also shown by the sharp drop in trade compared with the smaller drop in economic production in 2009.[6]

Boston Consulting Group research said that China's cost advantage over the U.S. in manufacturing will be closed within 5 years. It cited transportation, duties, supply-chain risks, and industrial real-estate costs as other factors that reduce the attractiveness of globally outsourced manufacturing.[7]

Small Towns Define What It Means To Be Local

Small towns are the definition of local, where culture is connected with a place. Each small town has its own identity and cultural flavor. Planned suburbs tend to resemble each other more than small towns, and strip malls are very similar, one to another, compared to the wide variety of shops in small towns. A strip mall in a Boston suburb and one in a Fort

Worth suburb can look very similar. The downtown business district of tiny Amesbury, Massachusetts, looks very different from the downtown business district of tiny Justin, Texas. Two small towns are more different than they are alike. That gives small town residents a stronger tie to a sense of place and their local culture.

There is a broad feeling that small towns are somehow part of the past; that they don't exist anymore. People from urban and suburban backgrounds can react with surprise when they suddenly face the fact that small towns are still here and thriving. Gary Vaynerchuk recognized the shift of business back to small town rules, but also said it was a return to the 1950s.[8] Except small towns didn't disappear in the 1950s. A travel poster in the Cincinnati airport in 2009 sported the tag line, "Experience Ohio's Small Town Past."[9]

The perception of small towns as part of the past gives people a sense of nostalgia about small towns. The small town has become the model of the ideal local place in the mind of Americans. When the Soul of the Community Project asked 43,000 people what made a community a desirable place to live, they found people wanted some typically small town characteristics: places to meet each other and take in entertainment, a feeling of openness and welcoming, and the physical beauty of a place, including green spaces. These desires are the same across the country and were stronger factors than even the economy or people's individual demographics.[10]

Shop local also began in small towns. Long before there were studies and national attention for this, small towns were promoting local shopping. They were at the center of the anti-chain store activity decades ago. More than 10 years ago, Hardtner, Kansas (population around 300), posted signs at the edge of town so that residents would see them as they left town. The signs said, "Did you really try to buy it in Hardtner?" Hundreds of other little "shop at home" promotions started from economic necessity in small towns all over, trying to retain more dollars in their local economy. Now that it's a national trend, larger businesses and national brands can examine what those small towns have learned by promoting "shop local."

The Small Town Rule: Build Your Local Connections

Small towns have embraced the local movement. Small town businesses thrive by maintaining their connection to their culture, their place and telling their story. The rules of successful shop local campaigns provide methods that businesses and brands can adapt when building local connections.

Connect with Your Culture and Place

Small towns have personality. Each one is different. From the maritime New England, to the outback of Australia, to the American prairie, each place has a history and a geography that influences the people, the businesses, and the culture. This culture permeates the best small town businesses. Any consumer can tell that L.L. Bean is from Maine. The Silver Barn antique store operates online, but it keeps its local Texas flavor.[11] Restaurants may be the best example of this. Themed restaurants, like Cracker Barrel, feature the culture and flavor of an area, even as they are franchised out far from the original location.

Smart entrepreneurs anywhere can connect with their local culture and place. For businesses in big cities, the local neighborhood is the source of local culture.

Businesses with more than one location have a choice to make: Adopt one culture and place to apply consistently across locations or work with the multiple places and adopt local culture.

One easy way to become part of the local culture is to connect with a local festival or fair. It seems every town or neighborhood has a festival, whether it's art, food, games, or just social. Every festival is always looking for sponsors and volunteers. Smart businesses get involved financially and personally.

To understand the culture of a local place, whether it's a small town, a suburb, or an urban neighborhood, the best place to start is the *8 Elements of Rural Culture* from the Kansas Sampler Foundation. Marci Penner developed these elements to help small towns get past the "there's nothing to do here" mental block. The elements are architecture, art, commerce, cuisine, customs, geography, history, and people. Any entrepreneur or brand can use these eight elements to better understand and build connection with their local culture.[12]

Using a Local Story to Build Engagement Like Milk

Local businesses enjoy a high level of engagement with their customers because they are located in the same community and have a higher chance for interaction. Because strong engagement is a characteristic that people associate with their local businesses, it is also one that any business can work to cultivate. There is a progression of engagement along a continuum. The further the business progresses along that continuum with its customers, the more valuable customers will perceive the business to be.

At the bottom or entry level, a business offers a commodity, such as fresh milk. Up one step, a business has an asset, such as ice cream made from that milk. Another step up is an experience, such as serving that ice cream in the business' own ice-cream parlor. Step up again, and the business can transform that experience into a renewal. At this level, the business and the customer work together to change something, such as buying ice cream because they know it supports the state's last working dairy cooperative that makes its own ice cream, such as Pride Dairy in Bottineau, North Dakota.[13] Diane Olson of Bottineau County Economic Development introduced Becky to this story over a scoop of Pride Dairy's juneberry ice cream. (Any great story is better with ice cream!)

Without geographic boundaries for getting what they want, people are now making choices by knowing the story behind their purchases. They want to know where products come from, how a company got started, and what a business is doing to make the world a better place. They are interested to hear that a winery is paying local farmers to plant more rhubarb for fruit wine, like Maple Ridge Winery in North Dakota. The fact that the local farmers then earn more from a small plot of rhubarb than acres and acres of wheat adds to the story.[14] People are fascinated to learn that Pride Dairy runs radio ads offering to buy wild juneberries from locals when it's time to make the juneberry ice cream.

Urban businesses can use their story to build engagement, too. Nuts.com (formerly NutsOnline.com) is an online food and candy retailer that grew out of a family business, the Newark Nut Company founded in 1929 in the Mulberry Street open-air market. In 1999, the company began selling online. The website sells products and prominently features the story of the business complete with family photos. The personal tone involves customers in the 80 years of family history and provides customers a compelling reason to choose Nuts.com over other, less personal sites.[15]

When people think their purchase is part of maintaining a way of life or supporting the local community, they want to be part of the story with that business. But first, the business has to tell them the story.

How to Build a Shop Local Campaign

This section starts with an introduction to shop local campaigns and research on whether they work. It then walks through how to create this type of campaign and measure its success. This section contains tips for small towns, big cities, and urban neighborhoods. Special suggestions for national brands looking to build local connections are also included.

Introduction to Shop Local

A shop local, or buy local, campaign is a way of building a sense of community, of giving people a meaningful cause to support, and generating more sales for a company. Small town businesses can use a shop local campaign to help boost their sales. Big brands and national corporations can use shop local elements to better connect with local culture while boosting sales.

Research from the Independent Business Forum shows that shop local campaigns increase sales in good times and can reduce declines in bad times.[16] There is an increasing "buy local" sentiment among consumers to help boost the economy. Many people are willing to pay a higher price to support this effort because of the value it adds. For example, an Ohio State University study observed that people shopping for local foods were knowingly spending almost twice as much for local produce as for the usual trucked-in produce.[17]

Just "being local" is not a winning advantage, but it can be an equalizing edge. Even with the higher stated preference to support local, businesses still have to give people a compelling reason to shop local by providing an outstanding experience or product. This means the business has to shop local, too, for business supplies and services. No business wants to be busily promoting a buy local campaign and have it come out that they are outsourcing important purchases to another town or even another country. This is what is called in the big city "bad business karma."

Local Meets Urban

Although some big cities create a single project to cover their entire metropolitan area, urban neighborhoods and businesses can also use these campaigns to support their "hyperlocal" economy. Local in a big city can mean one street or a section of town. In Chicago, there are buy local campaigns for the neighborhoods of Uptown, Lakeview, Lincoln Park, and Roscoe

Village. These neighborhoods vary from a few streets to several square miles. Each has its own Chamber of Commerce and community-based organizations. Many have summer festivals large enough that they close off the streets to make room for neighborhood celebrations.

Shop Local for National Brands

For brands, there is an opportunity to support local campaigns in markets where they have an important presence. Brands can also tell the story of their efforts to use locally produced products and local suppliers around their manufacturing or to demonstrate a strong tie to their local community. Another possibility would be to create customized local products, specific to a small region and sourced locally, to strengthen local ties.

Going further to benefit their local communities, brands can make their assets available to local businesses. Their people, their distribution systems, and their purchasing power can be a huge benefit for other local businesses. Each of these is a logical and an authentic connection to shop local projects.

Consumers decide what is local by looking for markers of quality. Local ingredients make a difference, but so do the stories. Brands trying to be authentically local should share stories of local sources and local production. The Hartman Group said this:

> It is important for manufacturers, marketers, and retailers to understand that quality markers, such as use of local ingredients and narratives of local production and origin, are factors that resonate most strongly with consumers when it comes to determining what is authentically local.[18]

Bank Local

With the collapse of some national banks and the backlash from the federal bailout of these banks, a local banking movement is starting to grow. Local community banks were less hit by the recession because many did not get stuck in questionable lending practices. The community banks that did not take as much risk in the subprime lending area leading up to the recession have fared better than the industry as a whole. They now have become the source for small business loans in their local community. The people who work there volunteer in the community. They enter floats in the homecoming parade. (When was the last time anyone saw the international megabank in a small town or neighborhood parade?)

A website called Move Your Money encourages people to shift their money to locally owned banks. The site includes bank rankings by Institutional Risk Analytics.[19] The idea proved popular and spread widely on social networks and received news media attention. In 2011, small business owner Kristen Christian started a "bank local" project called "Bank Transfer Day." Consumers were urged to move their bank accounts from mega-banks to local credit unions on November 5.[20] Consumers are starting to act on their "bank local" thinking.

More Multipliers

Shop local campaigns can be multiplied by promoting buy local for business-to-business transactions, doing group purchasing, adding a bonus for local bidders in government business, and including local governmental services like the post office or utilities. It can make a difference to the local economy, the community, and the community services.

Do Buy Local Campaigns Work?

Yes, buy local campaigns work! Here are the results of four studies and surveys on the effectiveness of shop local or buy local campaigns:

- Nationwide comparison of holiday sales. The Independent Business Forum (IBF) conducted a survey on buy local campaigns during the 2007 holiday season. It found that independent retailers in cities with a buy local campaign reported an average gain in sales of about 2 percent over 2006. Those in cities without a campaign saw an increase of less than 0.5 percent. The IBF repeated the study for the dismal 2008 holiday season. Independent retailers in shop local cites held their losses down. They were down only 3 percent, instead of the more than 5 percent decline where there was not a buy local project.[21]

- Think Local First, Bellingham, Washington. In 2006, a survey on Bellingham's 3-year long Think Local First program showed that 58 percent of residents had changed their behavior and were now more deliberate about choosing local, independently owned businesses first.[22]

- Buy Local, Portland, Maine. Portland's buy local project also generated measurable positive results. In a 2007 survey, more than 60 percent of businesses said so, citing improved customer loyalty and sales. Almost 75 percent said customers had told them that they are making an effort to do more or all of their shopping at locally owned businesses. Forty percent of businesses said they had gained new customers from the project.[23]

- Buy Local Philly. After a month-long pilot program in 2005, Buy Local Philly had made a difference. Surveys showed that one in six people were aware of the initiative, and 40 percent of those had been motivated to shop at an independent business as a result. More than half of the participating business owners who were surveyed said the project had made a positive impact on their business. That's after just one month.[24]

For more examples, see the Institute for Local Self-Reliance's New Rules Project. It includes materials from Local First in Utah, Keeping Louisville Weird, Austin Unchained, and many others.[25]

Is Shopping Locally Inefficient?

Occasionally, opponents of shopping locally will use any one of the oft-repeated arguments against it. Zachary Barowitz wrote "The Top 10 Reasons NOT to Buy Local," calling it a double-standard, saying that globalization is good, and labeling it smug and elitist.[26] Businesses considering a shop local project will want to read the response from Stacy Mitchell, the researcher with the New Rules Project. Mitchell provided research and documentation of the benefits of relatively self-reliant communities that "freely and fairly trade with one another."[27]

Some local projects manage to bring together shop local principles with greater economic efficiency. The Tulsa Metropolitan Chamber of Commerce noticed how many businesses were purchasing items or services that could also have been sourced locally. Businesses simply were not aware of potential local suppliers. The Chamber of Commerce started the "Let's Do Business Tulsa" project, designed to help match up local buyers with local sources. Its website now contains many success stories of businesses that got the item they needed, at the same quality, and saved money as well as reduced transportation costs. That increased efficiency makes a potent answer to claims that globalization is always more efficient. There is more about the "Let's Do Business Tulsa" project under Step 7, on how to multiply results from a shop local campaign.[28] In 2009, Thomas Industry Market Trends published a piece by David R. Butcher that covered both sides of the debate. Butcher concluded that, "A growing body of evidence indicates that 'buy local' campaigns are helping small businesses compete in an extremely challenging economic climate."[29]

Seven Steps to Building a Shop Local Project

Building a successful comprehensive shop local campaign is a big project. The seven steps laid out here can be adapted for small towns, local neighborhoods, or national brands. Each project has to adapt to the local character, because every town and neighborhood is a little different.

Step 1: Get Some Help

No one organization can do all the work alone, so the first step is to start gathering allies and workers. In a small town or neighborhood, the key volunteers will be the STP (the "Same Ten People" who do everything together). It's still worth reaching out to other business owners. A shop local project may generate interest from surprising groups. For projects drawing from a national brand staff, the working group should be somewhere between 5 and 15 people. For brands initiating a project, it's critical to get participation from local people outside of the company early in the process. A local project can't be a local project with no local people involved.

Step 2: Pick a Theme

The theme for the shop local project determines how people in the community will think of it. Something short and punchy is best. Common phrases are Buy Local, Shop Local, Homegrown, Think Local First, Stay Local, and Buy Close By. Incorporate the personality and best-known symbols of the local community. Waynoka, Oklahoma, is a town with strong ties to the railroad business. The town chose "On The Right Track" as its theme. "Keep Austin Weird" is more of a grassroots movement than a buy local effort, but the slogan builds on that city's reputation perfectly. In urban neighborhoods and big cities, the emphasis is likely to be on buying from independent local merchants rather than from chains. In small towns, the focus stays on shopping at all the local businesses instead of heading out of town. For a larger brand, it makes sense to connect with what the local community wants and emphasize the connections to the local community. When athletic shoe brand Converse opened a specialty retail store in New

York City, it brought its brand and star logo together with the local "I Love New York" slogan, and used "I *> NYC" as its local-connection theme.

Step 3: Promote the Most Powerful Local Benefits

There are lots of lists of the benefits to shopping locally. A quick Internet search will find top ten lists, long comprehensive lists, ones with lots of explanation, and ones with bullet points.

With so many different lists of reasons to shop local, a few of the best stand out. Here is a list of ten that can be customized for use in local campaigns:

1. Dollars you spend locally support vital public services in your town and county.

2. Your community is unique, and one-of-a-kind businesses are an integral part of the distinctive character. Local ownership ensures that important decisions are made locally by people who live in the community and will feel the impacts of those decisions.

3. You can grow a relationship with your local merchants. They can get to know you and cater to your preferences.

4. Local merchants care about and invest in your community. They donate part of your dollars back to local groups and charities.

5. Your local purchases support local jobs.

6. When you shop at one local merchant, you're supporting a whole host of other business. Banks, restaurants, and other businesses depend on a thriving retail sector.

7. Local stores are more accessible for everyone, from the elderly, vulnerable, and even young people and those without transportation.

8. You save money by shopping at home. You drive less, save time, and you'd be surprised how often the retail prices are lower, too.

9. You can reduce your environmental impact by cutting out those long drives to the big city.

10. Your purchases help the town attract new entrepreneurs and skilled workers. Towns that preserve their one-of-a-kind businesses and distinctive character are more successful in recruiting.

Any shop local campaign needs a short and a long version of the benefit list. Short bullet lists work on social networks, posters, and table tents. Longer explanations can go in newspaper articles, blog posts, or handout flyers. The list should suit the style of the community, and the reasons selected should be the ones most likely to motivate local residents.

Here are a few examples of powerful local benefits worth featuring:

- Support critical community services. Rural economic development expert Jack Schultz found a compelling shop local campaign example in Perkins, Oklahoma. The ad showed the local fire department with this caption: "Every time you shop in Perkins, three cents of every dollar goes to keep our city government running—including our Fire Department. When you spend your dollars elsewhere, your money goes to equip somebody else's Fire Department. Be smart. Shop Perkins first. It helps you and it helps your neighbors."[30] In Escondido, California, the city is partnering with the Chamber of Commerce to promote "Spend It! In Escondido" with a similar message:

  "Every taxable dollar spent in Escondido benefits important City-provided services like police and fire, senior services, libraries, street maintenance, street lights, and parks. Sales tax generated from Escondido transactions stays in Escondido (1% of gross taxable sales) and contributes to the quality of life you enjoy."[31] Any local community or neighborhood can adapt this idea with a list of local services supported by local purchases.

- Support the local economy. A shop local campaign can tell everyone in a town how important it is to buy local, but it is just like any other common advice. Everyone "knows" it, so people don't really change their behavior. One way to track how shopping locally makes a difference and get people to change shopping habits is to *make the money itself noticeable*. Pharmacist Danny Cottrell did an experiment in Brewton, Alabama. He gave his employees $700 bonuses using uncommon $2 bills. Everyone in town noticed as the $2 bills were spent at local merchants. People saved them to respend in town, and several visited merchants they had not been to before.[32] Many towns do a similar thing with local currencies. The Berkshires region in Massachusetts has BerkShares, one of the most famous local currencies. Many local Chambers of Commerce issue "chamber bucks" as a currency redeemable only at member merchants. Any shop local campaign can implement this, and the idea of "noticeable money" could work well for a national brand wanting to showcase its local impact.

- Save money and gas. Gasoline prices always seem to be on the rise. Many small town residents are accustomed to driving to the "big city" to shop, and many urban residents like to head to big suburban shopping areas, away from their local neighborhood. Most people seem to do it without really thinking about the effort and cost involved. A shop local project could remind the community about that cost and effort while promoting local merchants at the same time.

- Every neighborhood has assets. All small towns and neighborhoods have gaps, or holes in the bucket, where spending on a certain item has to go out of town or out of the area. Still, few people realize exactly what kind of shopping opportunities are available locally. Becky's friend, Jeanne Cole, routinely needed lawn-mower blades for her husband's lawn-care business. She was driving an hour one way to a big-box store to get them. But, when the big box was out of the right blade, in desperation, she called the local motorcycle dealer who also sells mowers and other parts. (A typical small town business!) Sure enough, he had the blades in stock and for less than the big box was charging. Every small town and neighborhood has stories like this, and they make compelling copy for shop local benefits.

Step 4: Create Just the Right Promotional Materials

Big cities go all out, making everything from promotional shopping bags to tee shirts to buttons and everything in between. For small town campaigns, the project will need to focus just on the few most effective items. Window signs can make the biggest splash, sparking discussion. Information sheets to put in customer bags at retail businesses can also gain attention quickly.

The next most effective tools include stickers for local products, tee shirts, local directories, and maps. Local coupon books, loyalty punch cards and buy local passports can also work and inject some fun.

For brands, this is a huge opportunity to cross-promote local products along with the brand's items. The local product gets greater exposure, and the brand benefits from the local connections.

Step 5: Kick Off with Events and Media Coverage

In a small town or urban neighborhood, the committee will know the local newspaper people, as well as how much coverage to expect from them. Usually, that means the committee writing their own stories, and delivering them straight to the paper. Because it is a small town, if there is any question about what to expect, any member of the working group can pick up the phone and ask. Radio and community TV are also good sources, if they are available. Most local talk shows are eager for guests. Remember, any local media outlet needs content, and many will take as much as the project can provide!

For larger-scale projects and big brands, the key is to treat each location as a separate neighborhood. No single solution or template will work. Customization is needed for each location.

Participating in existing local events is the second-best promotional tactic for shop local campaigns. The campaign can set up a special table at the local car show, rodeo, or craft show. Local merchants can cooperate and create special in-store events. Then, it's up to the working group to provide those materials it already created and help promote the events.

Local clubs, associations, and membership groups are an important connection in both small towns and urban neighborhoods. Most look for speakers and programs monthly. The promotional materials and the list of reasons to shop local make a good local emphasis program.

The results from Buy Local Philly showed that these two tactics worked best: direct outreach through events and press coverage. Positive press coverage was good, but *it turned out that negative press coverage was also good.* A scathing article calling the campaign "protectionist" and "elitist" generated a debate in various media outlets. Many residents reported that they remembered the campaign because they disagreed with the negative article. Advertising was much less effective.[33]

Whether for an urban neighborhood, a small town, or a brand, it's important to feature the campaign prominently on all partner websites. When Becky did extensive research on shop local projects, she was surprised by the number of towns that she personally knew had a campaign, but had zero information on their websites.

Another online tactic that can work well is a Facebook Page or Group. Almost every small town and neighborhood has many people on Facebook. The bonus is that the shop local campaign builds a network for community support that can be used for other community projects.

Step 6: Measure Success

No matter where the project takes place, measureable results matter. The project must show real results and will be required to adjust and improve over time. The way to do that is to get feedback through surveys. For brands, the resources to conduct surveys are probably readily at hand. For small towns and smaller urban neighborhoods, surveys may be more difficult. One source of inexpensive surveys to measure success is the local (or nearby) community college or university. Students in marketing, statistics, or public relations may be available at no cost or low cost to conduct surveys for a community project. Organizers can also use online survey tools, such as Zoomerang and Survey Monkey. Simple Facebook and LinkedIn polls can also be useful for quick feedback.

The standard of success for a shop local project is relatively modest. Researcher Dr. Pamela Jull said, "Normally, if 1 in 5 households claim familiarity with your program and change their behavior because of it, you would consider it a success."[34] For some reason, coming up with good survey questions is an arcane art. Success means thinking ahead about which information is the most important to gather that will yield actionable results. Many surveys waste effort by asking questions that don't matter or that won't be used to improve the project.

Here are some sample questions to help evaluate the success of a shop local project.

For residents:

- Are you aware of the campaign?
- Where did you hear or learn about the campaign?
- Have you changed your buying behavior because of it?
- Have you visited businesses where you don't normally shop?

- If you have spent more in town, how much more per month?
- What did you learn that surprised you during the campaign?
- What would you do differently, if you ran the program?

For businesses:

- Has the campaign benefited your business?
- If sales have increased, how much per month?
- Have customers mentioned the buy local campaign?
- Have you seen new customers?
- Would you recommend the program to other businesses?
- Would you recommend the program to other communities?
- Will you continue to participate?
- What would you do differently, if you ran the program?

It makes sense to conduct a survey at 3 months into the campaign and another after 1 year. If students are conducting the surveys, the timing will have to work with their class schedule.

Step 7: Multiply the Results

Encouraging community residents to increase their local purchasing is just one way to generate local results. There are several other aspects to promoting local commerce that can apply to brands, urban neighborhoods, and small towns. These include

- Promote buy local in business-to-business transactions. Consumers aren't the only ones doing the buying. There are also businesses making purchases in every local neighborhood. Capturing more of those purchases would provide another boost to the local economy. The Tulsa Metropolitan Chamber of Commerce sponsors a program of business-to-business buy local in their "Let's Do Business Tulsa" project. Participating companies pledge to do business with other local companies when possible. The chamber created an online database where local businesses can register their products and services, and other businesses can search for what they need. The project's goal is to bring 5 percent of the out-of-state spending by local businesses back to the local economy. There are more than 900 participating companies reviewing their purchasing and making offers to local suppliers first. One company, Metal Panels, Inc., said that it was able to improve its bottom line by bringing its printing and office-supply purchasing within the Tulsa metro area.[35]

- Do group purchasing for business. Group purchasing is an old concept that has gained a lot of new attention with new technology. Groupon was the most famous of the startups in the arena, with many more forming around the idea of being the "Groupon for small business." Brands working to improve a local economy may be able to build or tap into a group purchasing option for local merchants. A small town or urban-neighborhood project could coordinate group purchases of items local companies need, but can't purchase locally.

- Ask for a bonus for buying local in government purchases. For small towns, this could start with approaching the town council to adopt a policy to give a preference to local bidders in all kinds of purchasing. Salinas, California, gives local businesses rights of first refusal if the local bid is within 10 percent of a non-local bid.[36] It might be just as effective to take the time to remind the town council and town administrators about buying local at least every couple of months. Praising local leaders in public for buying local might also be effective. After all, many local leaders are also local merchants.

- Include critical local government services in the shop local project. One key to retaining local government services in an era of cutbacks is to increase their utilization. Shop local projects can also promote buying stamps at the local post office or encourage support for the local utilities and civic services. Many schools and educational groups offer services or products either as fundraisers or as projects. That is another logical target for a shop local project. This tactic can work just as well for small towns, urban neighborhoods, and brands.

- Help local businesses improve. Here is a great place for brands to get involved with other local businesses. Many local businesses could use training or assistance in improving their service to the community. Others could use some work on improving their physical location. Loaned executives or volunteer efforts to help and support local businesses can be incredibly positive. Groups of volunteers came together to help clean up, paint, and spruce up a favorite local cafe in Whiting, Kansas, and a treasured local independent grocery in Wilmore, Kentucky.[37] Brands can take the lead in creating improvement projects.

For small towns and urban neighborhoods, this is a chance to work with local businesses to earn more of that local business. Many local companies can use training and information that will help them to improve customer service, expand hours, and generally offer local customers what they want. Training may be available from the state Main Street program, the extension service, or from the nearest university.

- Become an exporter of business. Capturing more local sales is one way to create an increase. Capturing more sales from out of town is another. One small town business may be able to provide a service that an even smaller neighboring town could not support on its own or a neighborhood business may be able to cover a larger geographic area. In this area, brands might be able to use their existing distribution chain to help a local business reach markets further from home.

Conclusion

In this business environment, resources and volunteer hours are scarce. A shop local campaign can be particularly effective to help build the local economy of a small town or an urban neighborhood. All factors being equal, people say they want to buy from local sources. They want to buy from people they can see and talk to. This is one way to accomplish that goal.

For brands, working together to benefit the local economy is a strong way to build local ties and to be part of the local community. Brands can focus on using local products or create customized local products. Cooperating with local businesses can provide a big connection to the local economy. Also, brands must specifically tell the stories of their local efforts in order to connect with consumers.

Apply the Small Town Rule to Big Brands: How Brands Can Go Local

In the U.S., many people are originally from a small town no matter where they live now. This is why so many consumers connect with their "small town roots." Some big brands take advantage of this by simulating local roots as part of their "retail theatre" buying environment.

For example, Cracker Barrel's Old Country Store and Restaurant preserves its "simple" beginnings by constructing every outlet to appear like the original which was built in Lebanon, Tennessee, in 1969:

> What Dan Evins had in mind was the kind of place he'd been to hundreds of times as a boy. It was a place called the country store, something every small community once had. Out west, they called them trading posts; up north, they were general stores. Where Dan grew up, in Middle Tennessee, they were old country stores, and Dan figured maybe folks traveling on the big new highways might appreciate a clean, comfortable, relaxed place to stop in for a good meal and some shopping that would offer up unique gifts and self-indulgences, many reminiscent of America's country heritage.[38]

Although the concept was common across many geographic areas, Evins connected to his own local version and shared that in his business.

The stated goal for the company today is for "everyone who walks in our front door to get a warm welcome and a good meal at a fair price.... Things are likely to stay this way, too. Call it nostalgia if you want, but the goal isn't simply to recreate to a time gone by—it's to preserve it. Because the way we see it, the lifestyle of rural America isn't about where you live. It's about how you live."[39]

Extending that idea, local isn't just about where a business is based; it's about how it does business.

Even companies that lack a compelling local history can find ways to connect with the customer's idea of local ties. When anyone enters Einstein Bros. Bagels, they are struck with old photographs of the humble beginnings of the inventive Einstein brothers, Melvyn and Elmo. Unlike Cracker Barrel, this history is just the imagination of a branding company. The corporation was originally formed by Boston Chicken, Inc., in 1995, when it was looking to sell breakfast food.[40]

Another major brand with a small town beginning is Walmart. It had very small town beginnings in Rogers, Arkansas, in 1962, founded by Sam and Helen Walton. Its brand tries to maintain that friendly local feel today with greeters at every store. Now, with almost 10,000 stores, Walmart sticks with the same mission as described in Walton's autobiography:

> ...if you think about it from the point of view of the customer, you want everything: a wide assortment of quality merchandise; the lowest possible prices; guaranteed satisfaction; friendly, knowledgeable service; convenient hours; and a pleasant shopping experience. You love it when a store exceeds your expectations, and you hate it when a store inconveniences you, gives you a hard time, or pretends you're invisible.[41]

American consumers cheer humble beginnings. Ever since Bill Hewlett and David Packard founded Hewlett-Packard in 1939 in a Palo Alto, California garage, start-up entrepreneurs have been trying to duplicate their success. Other Fortune 500 companies that reportedly started in a garage include Apple and Mattel. This has become so popular that there are even start-up competitions that are staged in a garage.

Many big brands now emphasize local as part of their strategy. Whole Foods proudly promotes its dedication to local products and foods. To be called "local" by Whole Foods, a product must travel less than one day (7 hours or fewer by car or truck). Many individual stores have set even shorter limits for the "local" designation.[42]

Groupon only sells local deals. The brand has become known nationwide, but the consumers' experience is entirely focused on local businesses and local offers. In 2011, it launched Groupon Now, targeting consumers while they are mobile with local deals available immediately.[43] Review site Epinions went from national to local with a new site, Nextdoor, designed as a private social network for individual neighborhoods. Members have to verify they live within a neighborhood to join. The same kind of discussions that people used to share face to face can be shared online. Recommendations of local service providers, like plumbers or babysitters, are joined by discussions of neighborhood issues. This may serve as a social network well-suited to suburbs. Other natural social networks are better suited for rural areas or dense urban neighborhoods, so suburbs have been harder to serve socially.[44]

Dex One is a marketing-solutions company that comes from the world of printed telephone directories, an intensely local business. Today, the company leverages local market intelligence gathered from representatives in every one of its local markets. The representatives get to know the local similarities and the regional differences as Dex continues to focus on local businesses. Far more than just printed directories, Dex One now offers online local search, mobile search with local data, and an online ad network.[45]

Fairfield Inn is another national brand going local. The 670-hotel chain is customizing its properties to reflect local cultural elements. For example, the Fairfield Inn in Washington's Chinatown reopened in March 2011 with red lantern light fixtures and a large mural with a dragon in the lobby. In Santa Cruz, California, the local Fairfield sports a 400-pound giant jellyfish chandelier.[46]

Summary: The Local Movement Is Here

Local flavor is the antidote to a bland national character. The local movement is undermining the creation of a single, monolithic culture for everyone, and replacing parts of it with local food, local business, and local taste. Often, it's a taste of small town culture that is being appreciated once again by consumers.

The Small Town Rule: Build Your Local Connections

The corollaries:

1. Connect with your culture and place. Every business comes from someplace. Rather than drop that local culture to try to fit a homogeneous national culture, successful businesses and brands can retain their culture. There has never been a better time to flaunt a regional accent.

2. Use a local story to build engagement. Every place has a story...or lots of stories. By looking through the eight elements of the local culture, businesses can better understand and can start telling the stories that customers will connect with.

3. Build a shop local campaign. Now that "shop local" is on the mind of every consumer, campaigns and projects can grow tremendously. Small towns, urban neighborhoods and national brands all have the opportunity to forge local connections that matter and build a stronger local economy.

A Look Ahead

The trends leading in to the local movement have been decades in the making. Now that those trends have collided and started reshaping the local fabric, they aren't going away soon. Young people are buying more real estate in walkable neighborhoods, and the Occupy Wall Street protests against national corporations have spilled into local neighborhoods all over America. Each local protest is even named for the local area, like Occupy Carbondale or Occupy Dallas. All these different facts point to the same conclusion: Local is here to stay.

Resources for Implementing the Small Town Rules

Given the wide range of subjects touched on in *Small Town Rules*, it is not possible to go into complete depth on every one of them. These resources mentioned in this appendix provide additional information to help big brands and small businesses put the rules and corollaries into practice.

Note that resource information changes frequently, so check this book's website, www.smalltownrules.com, for the latest.

Chapter 1: Surviving Difficult Economic Times for the Big and Small

Be Prepared for Disasters and Other Situations That May Come or Not Happen at All!

Ready.gov (www.ready.gov/business/). Suitable for large businesses to develop a preparedness program, emergency response plan, and business continuity plan.

Small Business Administration (www.sba.gov/content/disaster-preparedness). Suitable for small businesses, with extensive links and information, including government disaster assistance to small businesses.

Office Depot Disaster Preparedness Kit (www.officedepot.com/promo.
do?file=/promo/disaster/main.jsp). Suitable for small businesses. Provides
statistics to help motivate planning and provides simple outlines for preparing plans.

**"Disaster Preparedness and Business Continuity Planning at Boeing: An
Integrated Model."** *Journal of Facilities Management*. July 2004. Detailed
profile by Carolyn Castillo of a large business developing a robust business
continuity plan.

The Worst Hard Time. **Egan, Timothy.** Boston: Houghton Mifflin Co.,
2006.

Reader's Guide for *The Worst Hard Time* (http://hmhbooks.com/
readers_guides/egan_worst.shtml). This interview with Timothy Egan
includes explanation of the relevance of the Dust Bowl for today's disasters.

Data Backup Tools. Services such as Carbonite (www.carbonite.com/) and
Mozy (http://mozy.com/) constantly back up computer files whenever an
Internet connection is available.

Backupify (www.backupify.com). Backup service for social networks. It
stores backup copies of social data online and allows downloading.

Question Assumptions

Creative Think by Roger von Oech (www.creativethink.com/). Excellent resources on creative thinking, including several books and tools. The
article "Think Like a Wise Fool" (http://blog.creativethink.com/2011/08/
think-like-a-wise-fool.html) breaks down different methods of questioning
assumptions. App for iPhone and iPad "Creative Whack Pack" (http://blog.
creativethink.com/2010/09/new-creative-whack-pack-app-for-ipad-iphone.
html) spurs creative thinking.

Top Creativity News (http://creativity.alltop.com/). Alltop pulls together
stories from the top sites on the subjects of creativity and creative thinking
into a virtual magazine rack.

"Question Inbuilt Assumptions" (www.jackcanfield.com/media-center/
community-videos/95-jack-canfield/video/165-tim-ferriss-a-jack-canfield-
share-secrets-to-success-qquestion-inbuilt-assumptionsq.html). Short video
from Jack Canfield and Tim Ferriss provides insight on how to question
assumptions.

Know the Seasons and Cycles

"Concise Encyclopedia of Economics" (www.econlib.org/library/Enc/ BusinessCycles.html). An article on business cycles by Christina D. Romer.

"How to Uncover Your Business' Unique Sales Cycle" (http:// womengrowbusiness.com/2011/01/how-to-uncover-your-business-unique-sales-cycle/). Article by Suzanne Paling targeted at small businesses, but useful for any size brand.

"Business Seasonality and Search Trends for Your Marketing" (www.ecommerce-blog.org/archives/business-seasonality-and-search-trends-for-your-marketing/). An article on using Google search trends to analyze seasonality by Jamie Estep.

"How Seasonality Interacts with the Business Cycle" (http://ideas.repec. org/p/man/cgbcrp/09.html). Research paper by Denise Osborn.

Chapter 2: The New Normal: Profiting When Resources Are Limited

Be Frugal in Every Business

The Lean Startup: How Today's Entrepreneurs Use Continuous Innovation to Create Radically Successful Businesses. **Ries, Eric.** New York: Crown Business, 2011. This book shares practical experience in applying frugality to startup businesses.

Startup Lessons Learned (www.startuplessonslearned.com/). Website by Eric Ries with ongoing coverage of lean startup ideas.

"First Break All the Rules" (www.economist.com/node/15879359). Cover story on "frugal innovation" from big brands and small businesses and how it affects product design, business plans, production processes, and manufacturing processes. *Economist*, April 17, 2010.

"Frugal Is Back" (www.entrepreneur.com/article/200102). Article by Tiffany Meyers on making small businesses more efficient, including examples from successful entrepreneurs. *Entrepreneur,* March 2009.

"Restructuring for the 'New' Normal" (www.financialexecutives.org/ KenticoCMS/Financial-Executive-Magazine/2009_07/strategy--july-2009. aspx). Article on the steps large firms can take to reposition for the current economic environment and the future, including frugality, alternative financing, and customer service.

Creative Financing

Locavesting: The Revolution in Local Investing and How to Profit From It. **Cortese, Amy.** New Jersey: John Wiley & Sons. 2011. Contains information on alternative financing, including community development financial institutions (CDFI), direct public offerings (DPO), cooperatives, and crowdfunding.

Startup Accelerator Programs (www.youtube.com/watch?v=l0NfRN730ts). Accelerators are usually set up by small groups of investors to educate founders on the basics of starting a high-growth potential business. Some offer investor funding or other services. The video, "What is a Startup Accelerator?" by PBS Newshour, explains more. Listing of seed stage startup accelerator programs: (http://blog.shedd.us/321987608/).

Business incubators (www.nbia.org/links_to_member_incubators/). A listing of business incubators from National Business Incubator Association. Incubators provide a wide range of services, sometimes including financing or tax incentives, to startup and early-stage companies. Business incubators can be found all over the world in major metropolitan areas and small towns.

Kansas Capital Funds Programs Map (http://apps.kda.ks.gov/GIS/ks_cap.cfm#). Every state has some capital funds, special loan programs, and other interesting business financing tools. Most are available only in some locations, and many that are widely available, like USDA funding, have different contact people in different places. Kansas put it all on a map.

The Complete Idiot's Guide to Crowdsourcing. **Sherman, Aliza.** New York: Alpha Books. 2011. Chapter 20 introduces fundraising from crowds, including peer-to-peer lending, project fundraising, and for-profit funding.

Creative Brand Management

Creative Brand Management (www.brandcenter.vcu.edu/9.aspx#creative-brand). Virginia Commonwealth University (VCU) degree program brings together the creative side of brands with the management side.

Lindstron, Martin. "Don't Hurt Your Brand While You're Cutting Costs," *Asia's Media & Marketing Newspaper,* March 23, 2007. Editorial on cutting marketing costs while using creative brand management to keep brand awareness high.

Top Branding News (http://branding.alltop.com). Alltop pulls together stories from top branding sites into a virtual magazine rack.

Chapter 3: Adapting to the New Economic Realities of Self-Reliance

Managing Multiple Lines of Income

While We're Talking About Branding (http://shiftingcareers.blogs. nytimes.com/2007/11/28/while-were-talking-about-branding/). Article by Marci Alboher includes advice from seasoned coach and writer Pam Slim on managing "slash" or multiple careers or brands.

"Managing Multiple Businesses" (www.businessweek.com/smallbiz/ content/apr2010/sb2010045_646630.htm). An article featuring advice from four serial entrepreneurs written by Karen E. Klein.

"4 Ways to Manage Multiple Businesses" (www.smallbizsurvival.com/ 2010/01/4-ways-to-manage-multiple-businesses.html). An article by Becky McCray featuring multiple-business advice from entrepreneurs captured during #SBBuzz Twitter Chat, organized into four themes.

Renaissance Woman: Managing Multiple Businesses Like It's Your Job, 'Cause It Is (www.taragentile.com/managing-multiple-businesses/). Advice by Tara Gentile on finding the core mission to multiple solo-preneur businesses.

Selling Expertise Online

Differences in Distance Learning and In-Person Learning (www.uiweb. uidaho.edu/eo/dist1.html). University of Ohio Engineering Outreach published this guide to Distance Education at a Glance.

A variety of learning/teaching platforms:

Litmos (www.litmos.com) platform

Prfessor (www.prfessor.com/) platform and community

Digital Chalk (www.digitalchalk.com/) platform

WizIQ (www.wiziq.com/) platform and community

Odijoo (www.odijoo.com/) platform

Teaching Sells (http://teachingsells.com/). Course and membership forum on educating online as a business. Enrollment opens during limited periods.

Top eLearning News (http://elearning.alltop.com). Alltop pulls together stories from top eLearning sites into a virtual magazine rack.

Brand Extension

Annual Brand-Extension Survey (www.brandchannel.com/papers_review. asp?sp_id=1222). Survey from Brandchannel in collaboration with *Brandweek* magazine names best and worst brand extensions in eight popular categories.

The 4 Dangers of Brand Extension (http://neutronllc.com/ideas/ dangers_of_brand_extension). Marty Neumeier discusses four issues to be considered when leveraging an existing brand.

The Asymmetric Effects of Extending Brands to Lower and Higher Quality. Heath, Timothy B., Devon DelVecchio, and Michael S. McCarthy. July 2011. *Journal Of Marketing* 75. Research report shows that brand extensions improve brand valuation. Medium-quality brands can gain by adding both higher- and lower-quality line extensions.

The Wheel of Retailing Revisited: Toward a Wheel of e-Tailing (www.aabri.com/manuscripts/11838.pdf). Massad, Victor J., Mary Beth Nein, Joanne M. Tucker. Research paper applies the Wheel of Retailing theory to online sellers. September 2011. *Journal of Management and Marketing Research.*

Chapter 4: Adapting to the "Anywhere, Anywhen" Business World

Work Anywhere

Microsoft Study, "Work Without Walls" (www.microsoft.com/presspass/ features/2011/may11/05-18workwithoutwalls.mspx). This survey finds a rise in the number of companies offering employees opportunities to work remotely.

National Dialogue on Workplace Flexibility (www.dol.gov/wb/media/
natldialogue3.htm). The U.S. Department of Labor has made workplace
flexibility a priority issue. This list of reports and publications includes
resources for improving workplace flexibility.

Fortune Magazine 100 Best Companies to Work For (http://money.cnn.
com/magazines/fortune/bestcompanies/2011/benefits/telecommuting.
html). Eighty-two of the best companies, that allow employees to telecom-
mute or work at home at least 20 percent of the time are listed.

Winning Workplaces (www.winningworkplaces.org/library/index.php).
Helps small and mid-sized organizations create high-performance workplaces through workplace best practices.

Workshifting (http://workshifting.com/). Provides ongoing coverage of
telework and related trends and tools for shifting where, when, and how
work is done. From Citrix Online.

Work Anywhen

The Anywhen Manifesto by Chris Brogan (www.chrisbrogan.com/
the-anywhen-manifesto/). Brogan declares war on those who threaten anywhen: "the state that the Internet provides us by allowing me to write this
when I want and you can consume it when you want."

"Making Anywhen a Possibility" (www.awayfind.com/blog/2010/03/
making-anywhen-a-possibility/). Article by Jared Goralnick responding to
Brogan's "anywhen" posts.

AwayFind (www.awayfind.com/). Digital assistant that finds and delivers
only urgent emails.

Rural Sourcing

Building IT Capabilities in Rural America (www.emeraldinsight.com/
journals.htm?issn=1753-8297&volume=3&issue=3&articleid=1896491&
show=html). Report by Mary Lacity, Joseph Rottman, and Shaji Khan on
the rural sourcing trend in 2010.

Rural America OnShore Outsourcing (www.ruralamericaonshore.com/
resources/resources-at-rural-america). Collection of white papers,
webinars, and other educational materials about onshoring.

Cross USA (www.cross-usa.com/news/news.htm#). White papers on rural sourcing.

LinkedIn group: Alternatives to Off-Shore (www.linkedin.com/groups?gid=1435167&trk=myg_ugrp_ovr). Cross USA's John Beesley organized this list.

Rural Sourcing, Inc (www.ruralsourcing.com/). Presentation on rural sourcing. It lacks explanations or speaker's notes, but still offers useful information. Find it under "Insights" on the Rural Sourcing, Inc., homepage.

"Rural Outsourcers' Vie for Offshoring Dollars" (www.businessweek.com/smallbiz/content/sep2010/sb20100922_365099.htm). Nick Leiber profiles several rural sourcing firms in this Bloomberg Businessweek article.

"Forget India, Outsource to Arkansas" (http://money.cnn.com/2010/07/08/smallbusiness/rural_onshoring/index.htm). Jennifer Alsever profiles rural sourcing firms and discusses their impact in this CNN Money article from 2010.

Chapter 5: Forget Advertising: Learn Customer-Driven Communication

Treat Customer Service as All You've Got

Cluetrain Manifesto (www.cluetrain.com/). The Manifesto by Chris Locke, Doc Searls, David Weinberger, and Rick Levine declares, "A powerful global conversation has begun. Through the Internet, people are discovering and inventing new ways to share relevant knowledge with blinding speed. As a direct result, markets are getting smarter—and getting smarter faster than most companies." This site is a place where it all started.

BAM! Bust A Myth, Delivering Customer Service in a Self Service World. Moltz, Barry J. and Mary Jane Grinstead. Bloomington, Indiana: AuthorHouse, 2009. When almost everything is a commodity, this book shows how customer service is the new marketing.

American Express 2011 Global Customer Service Barometer (http://about.americanexpress.com/news/docs/2011x/AXP_2011_csbar_market.pdf). Survey measures customer feelings about the current state of customer service, as well as how much more customers will spend to get excellent service.

Dell Social Media Listening Command Center (http://en.community. dell.com/dell-blogs/direct2dell/b/direct2dell/archive/2010/12/08/dell-s-next-step-the-social-media-listening-command-center.aspx) An example of a big company that takes social-media listening seriously. Dell's Lionel Menchaca describes the project.

Top Customer Service News (http://customer-service.alltop.com). Alltop pulls together stories from top customer service sites into a virtual magazine rack.

Use Social CRM Tools to Connect with Customers

These Customer Relationship Management (CRM) tools allow businesses to maintain better connections with customers as individuals. Note that these tools change constantly. Personal research is strongly encouraged.

Rapportive (http://rapportive.com). Free browser add-on that displays a sidebar in Gmail that shows the sender's picture, companies, and other networks where they can be found online. Users can add private notes about contacts.

Xobni (http://xobni.com). Provides similar functions to Rapportive for Gmail, Outlook, and mobile users. Contacts show up in the Xobni sidebar with pictures and links to their other networks. Related app Smartr maintains synchronized and enhanced contacts across multiple platforms.

Gist (http://gist.com). One place to keep all social-contact information together. Pulls contacts from email address books and social networks. Allows exploration of more information on contacts, other social presences, and monitoring of their updates. Sends email summaries of those contacts' activities.

BatchBook (http://batchblue.com). Integrates contacts from different places, pulling in their social network profiles and blog feeds. Brings together different team members with shared data. Logs different kinds of communication with customers in one place. Integrates with other small business-related services, like Freshbooks and MailChimp.

HiRise HQ (http://highrisehq.com). CRM for small business by the creators of Basecamp; this CRM tool is designed to be "stupid-proof." Organizes email conversations and notes, tracks proposals, and shares information across teams.

Chapter 6: How Big Brands and Small Businesses Are Thinking and Acting Small

Build Community

Online Community Management for Dummies. **Ng, Deborah**. New York: John Wiley & Sons, 2011. In-depth guide to building community online for businesses, written by an experienced community manager.

Online Community Management for Dummies online "cheat sheet" (http://www.dummies.com/how-to/content/online-community-management-for-dummies-cheat-shee.html). This online article by Deborah Ng includes do's and don'ts of engaging community.

Twitter chats. Major small business-related chats include #smbiz on Tuesday nights and #smallbizchat on Wednesday nights. Industry-specific chats cover a wide range, such as #agchat, #carchat, and #eyeconnect (eye-care professionals). Business specialties are also represented, such as #aopm (product management), #brandchat (branding), and #innochat (innovation). A useful list of Twitter chats is maintained by volunteers at http://bit.ly/ChatSched. To participate in the chats, tools like TweetChat (www.tweetchat.com/) and Twitterfall (www.twitterfall.com/) are currently recommended.

Online Community Guidelines for Brands

The Coca-Cola Company Online Social Media Principles (www.thecoca-colacompany.com/socialmedia/). Short guidelines considered a model in the industry.

New Media and the Air Force (www.af.mil/shared/media/document/AFD-090406-036.pdf). 23 pages of guidelines, including social media, blogging, guidelines, metrics, engagement, tips, and examples in action.

"Five Things the Air Force Knows About Social Media That You Should Too" (http://spinsucks.com/social-media/five-things-the-air-force-knows-about-social-media-that-you-should-too-seriously/). Article by Arment Dietrich includes graphic version of how to respond to blog posts following Air Force guidelines.

Best Buy Guidelines for Online Interaction (http://forums.bestbuy.com/t5/Welcome-News/Best-Buy-Social-Media-Policy/td-p/20492). "Be smart.

Be respectful. Be human." Short guidelines provide what to do and what not to do online.

Online Database of Social Media Policies (http://socialmediagovernance. com/policies.php). As of this writing, links to policies from 194 organizations were included.

Small Business Resources

American Express Open Forum (www.openforum.com/). Open Forum is a large and active site. Dozens of business experts and well-known entrepreneurs write original content on a wide variety of topics. Each topic includes videos, articles, and discussions, making it easy to learn about a specific area. Some features, including the forum discussions, are for AmEx cardholders only. (Disclosure: Barry writes for Open Forum.)

Small Business Trends: (www.smallbiztrends.com). This site is a source of information, news, and advice covering small business market issues. It offers a variety of resources to keep the small business owner informed daily. Each year, it publishes a series of articles on the upcoming trends in many different industries and specialties.

Marketing Matters and Shop Talk–DexOne (http://marketingmatters. dexone.com and http://shoptalk.dexone.com/social/). Marketing Matters includes marketing advice targeted to local businesses. News and stories about marketing are filtered through a lens of what works for local businesses. The Dex Ideas special reports on marketing ("29 Tips to Stretch Your Marketing Mileage," for example) are practical and useful for local business. Shop Talk focuses on social-media marketing. Social Glossary defines ever-changing terms used in social media. Tools and Apps/Social App Center provides a selected list of tools and applications for local businesses to make the most of social-media marketing. (Disclosure: Barry speaks for DexOne at local events.)

Visa Business Network (www.visabusinessnetwork.com/). This site has a primary emphasis on interactive features of goals, networking, and answers, rather than just articles to read. The goals combine step-by-step instruction with a to-do checklist through finishing the goal. The Network section includes both peers and mentors, so there are open discussions and more structured interaction. The Question and Answer feature is fairly professional in tone, with some serious business questions and excellent people providing answers. Articles are pulled from business magazines and small business blogs and websites. (Disclosure: Becky's blog is featured at the Visa Business Network Library.)

SmallBusiness.com (http://smallbusiness.com/wiki). A wiki for small businesses, which means everyone can participate in building the content. This project is spearheaded by Rex Hammock, a small business owner in Tennessee. Rex believes that together, small business people can put together some of the most relevant contextual content for each other. It contains user contributed how-to guides, local resource lists, and directories of small business blogs. One topic that Becky frequently gets questions about, exporting, has an excellent introduction entry: http://smallbusiness.com/wiki/Exporting_basics, with links to the SBA's guide on exporting. The Glossaries are also useful, such as the Accounting Glossary with more than 60 entries: http://smallbusiness.com/wiki/Category:Accounting_glossary.

Small Business Brief (www.smallbusinessbrief.com/). This is a small independent site. The tag line is "Fetching the best small business news," and it does it by providing links to selected small business articles from all around the web. Original articles are also featured. An active online community forum discusses marketing online and offline, insurance and taxes, ideas, and consulting business.

BizSugar (www.bizsugar.com/). This is a social-news site focused on small businesses. BizSugar users submit small business stories, and vote on those submitted by others. Those with the most votes are featured on the home page. The stories are divided by topics, and include short comments or reviews by users. Although there is no original content here, it is a good guide to finding some of the best recent content on a topic.

Intuit Small Business (http://blog.intuit.com/). Intuit is familiar to many small businesses because it publishes QuickBooks software. In addition, it publishes a small business blog with different categories than the usual set: Money, Inner Circle, Employees, Trends, and Local. It also has a Community section with a focus on Q&A.

CBS Interactive Business Network (http://www.cbsnews.com/money-watch/small-business/). Like many news-agency sites, it seems focused on current stories, without much easy access to archives. The quality of articles is excellent, however, so it's a good place to keep up-to-date on business news.

Business on Main–MSN (http://businessonmain.msn.com/). The special strength of Business on Main is video. It offers original videos on small business subjects, all the way to closing down a business. The tools and tips include practical templates and checklists.

Top Small Business News (http://small-business.alltop.com). Alltop pulls together stories from top small business sites into a virtual magazine rack. (Disclosure: Both Becky and Barry's sites are listed on Alltop Small Business.)

Business Owner's Toolkit (www.toolkit.com/). Professionals in the tax business probably already know the publishing firm CCH. Besides its comprehensive tax manuals, it has created a first-class resource site for small businesses, The Business Owner's Toolkit. It is full of excellent articles on all aspects of small business. Business Tools include model business documents (sample letters, contracts, forms, and policies ready to customize, from a sample Independent Contractor Agreement to a Job Application Form), financial spreadsheet templates (help for managing business finances, from balancing a checkbook to creating financial statements), checklists (information at a glance, from qualifying for the home office write-off to the right things to do and say during an employee termination interview), and official government forms (a selection of the forms and publications most commonly used by small business owners when filing taxes with the IRS or contracting with the federal government).

Chapter 7: Going Local, Even When You Are Big

Shop Local Resources

New Rules Project (www.newrules.org/). This site includes many resources on shop local campaigns.

The 3/50 Project (http://www.the350project.net/). This project encourages shoppers to pick three independently owned local businesses and spend $50 each month there.

Shop Small Saturday (http://smallbusinesssaturday.com/). The annual Small Business Saturday is a day established by American Express dedicated to supporting small businesses on one of the busiest shopping weekends of the year. They ask millions of people to shop small at local stores to help fuel the economy.

8 Elements of Rural Culture from the Kansas Sampler Foundation (www.kansassampler.org/rce/). Build local connections by better understanding the local culture, whether rural or urban.

Applying the 8 Elements of Rural Culture (www.smallbizsurvival. com/2010/01/developing-small-town-tourism.html). Becky McCray used Okeene, Oklahoma (population 1,240) as an example of applying the 8 Elements of Rural Culture from the Kansas Sampler Foundation.

Expion Software (http://expion.com/). Software for managing social-media profiles for brands with a local focus. The brand can centrally monitor, suggest content, and support local profiles.

"Brands to Focus on Localized Content Marketing." (www.marketingprofs .com/charts/2011/6295/brands-to-focus-on-localized-content-marketing). Article summarizing a study by the CMO Council on national marketers' use of localized marketing in traditional and online channels.

"Local Strategies in Retail." (http://trendwatching.com/trends/). Trend Watching give examples of retail businesses following the local trend. 2011 Retail Renaissance: scroll down to trend 16, "Limited Locations" (http:// trendwatching.com/trends/retailrenaissance/); 2010: scroll down to subtrend "Limited Locations" (http://trendwatching.com/trends/10trends2010/ #fluxury).

Business Ideas Inspired by the Small Town Rules

The small town rules represent a way of doing business that now applies to all businesses, no matter the size. This also means that all companies can learn from the types of business ideas that have worked well in small towns. Urban businesses and big brands can learn from this list of business ideas in four specific ways:

- **Improvement.** Every business, every day, can improve. Brands and businesses can be on the lookout for ideas that give a different point of view. This is where ideas for improvement and increased profit are often found.
- **Innovation.** The marketplace is constantly changing and innovating. The most successful business people filter all the ideas they hear and create an innovative new approach to doing business.
- **Expansion.** It is always easier to expand a business than to start a new one. Brands and small business can use these business ideas to complement their existing business in a direction they never thought about before.
- **Change the game.** A new business idea or execution of an old one can change, completely shifting a dominant paradigm.

Given all the change that has washed over the economy, technology, and society, it's time for some new ideas in business. These business ideas all spring from one of the small town rules and may provide the new direction any business needs.

Rule 1: Plan for Zero

Planning for zero income requires building new sources of revenue. For businesses with the right kind of community support, memberships may be an option. Government contracts can also help provide more predictable income.

Use Memberships to Support a Business

For businesses with wild swings in income, memberships are one way to level revenue out. One independent bookseller using this idea was profiled on NPR's Marketplace. Customers pay $20 to $2,500 in membership. What they receive is the knowledge that they are supporting the store's survival, although they also receive discounts and members-only event invitations. The bookstore raised more than $200,000 with memberships, which helped the store survive.[1] Any business with strong customer loyalty can use this idea to support its business through lean times and plan for those zero months and years.

Leverage Government Contracts to Average Out Lean Times

Securing government contracts can help support a business through the ups and downs of the commercial sector. For small businesses, state or local organizations may provide support or training to compete for government projects. Oklahoma's is called the Oklahoma Bid Assistance Network.[2]

For small businesses working on technology development, the Small Business Innovation Research (SBIR) program offers a way in to government grants. Eleven different federal agencies offer SBIR grants to companies that are solving a problem that the agency has a strong interest in. The federal agency gets a license for using the technology, and there are other conditions. The SBIR funding does help small businesses get through the zero years while developing a new technology.[3]

Rule 2: Spend Brainpower Before Dollars

Spending brainpower before spending dollars requires creativity. Businesses that get creative can develop an experience that will draw customers to them, and many times even act as an unexpected source of supplies and income.

Hotter Than Hell Night

Great business and promotion ideas don't have to cost a lot. Jim Storer describes the East Coast Grill in Cambridge, Massachusetts, that holds a huge destination event: Hotter Than Hell night. The entire night is eagerly awaited with crowds gathering in advance. People drive for miles and miles to get there. Servers dress in firefighter gear. Every dish on the menu is horrendously hot. The grill offers "food for wimps" and even an antidote, for a small "wimp charge."[4] The key to this idea is creating an event and a memorable experience for customers.

Fix Things and Resell Them

For individual business people, this is a chance to buy damaged items from online auction sites, repair them, and then resell the goods. This is most effective by specializing and focusing only on items that have a strong resale market.

For larger businesses and brands, tough economic times and more frugal consumers mean a new market for items that previously would have been discarded as damaged or not perfect. Land's End has done this for years with its Not Quite Perfect™ sales of items with tiny flaws, overstocks, wrong monograms, and colors that just were not a hit with customers.

For any business, honesty is essential. All repairs or flaws must be disclosed when the items are sold.

Becky got this idea from a student in one of her eBay classes. She would search eBay for broken china dolls. Her search keywords included "needs help" and "poor thing." These broken dolls came at a steep discount. She would repair and restore them, then offer them back for sale on eBay, where the market for those dolls was strong.

Rule 3: Build Multiple Lines of Income

To multiply the lines of income in a business, look at existing knowledge and assets in new ways. Every business has some assets that can be leveraged into new revenue streams.

Share Knowledge and Skills as a Taxi

Any business with training services could broaden its lines of income by offering a more in-depth type of coaching, like a tango taxi where teachers take students and learners out of the classroom and into the culture.

Author Robert Fulgham[5] reports that in the world of Buenos Aires tango, these special coaches are called taxis. They travel with learners out of the studio for an evening of dance at the learner's level and help them advance some in their skills. The difference between the taxi and the coach, trainer or teacher, is the setting. The best learning happens in an activity out in the world. Fulgham suggested applying this same concept to ballet, art museums, jazz, baseball, and singing.

The idea of a taxi-coach works well with tourism and culture. Rather than show visitors a static museum of western heritage, go with them to the field and help them learn the way of life by doing.[6]

Create Reference Guides

Any business with knowledge useful for beginners can create reference guides. Creating and selling eBooks and downloadable white papers gets a lot of attention in the online world, but there is still a place for printed learning guides. Who would be interested? Students, professionals, or people new to a particular field could benefit from printed and laminated guides like those created by BarCharts.[7] Guides could be customized and marketed to bookstores, business associations, and directly to students.

Share Building Space and Creativity

Old buildings or structures that aren't otherwise useful may make room for another business to co-locate, creative conference space, or artistic residences.

Businesses with extra space can allow another business, or several, to co-locate with them. In Ferdinand, Indiana (population 2,100), an entire community of businesses has opened in the same space at 1440 Main Street. They are able to support each other with promotions, sharing customers, and splitting expenses. There is also built-in networking between the co-located businesses.[8] This works in urban areas, too. Chicago-based crowdSPRING started out in co-located offices with a design firm.

Harveyville, Kansas (population 267), is repurposing old school buildings for creative conference space and artist residences. Short workshops and day-long events are leading up to longer residence programs. They provide opportunities for student and professional artists, writers, and musicians. Their Yarn School draws fiber artists from across the country to the tiny community. Other events on the schedule include encaustic painting, felt and fiber, and a cheese-making school.[9]

Upstairs Downtown

Another creative use for unused assets involves upstairs space. Many small towns have unused upstairs space in their downtown. One use for these spaces is non-traditional housing targeting younger residents. Young real estate buyers are shifting away from big suburban homes and toward smaller spaces in walkable neighborhoods.[10] Compliance with municipal codes and zoning can be an expensive challenge when converting downtown spaces for residential use.[11]

A local resident in Buffalo, Oklahoma (population 1,300), has used some of that space to create short-term lodging for hunters. Julia Hinther runs a salon and gift shop. The space upstairs used to be an apartment for her sons. When one of her sons tried his luck with guided hunts, they used the apartment to lodge the hunters. Her son is no longer guiding, but Julia is still renting the upstairs space to hunters. She markets it only by word of mouth, and has it booked up for hunting season every year. The rest of the time, she just rents it nightly to people needing a night's lodging in town. Interestingly, the nightly renters cause less damage to the property than when it was rented out monthly. And the pay back has been better, too.

Rule 4: Work Anywhere, Anywhen Through Technology

With the loss of geographic advantage, businesses can look outside the usual limits and boundaries. Technology allows more types of companies to reach customers anywhere and "anywhen."

Deliver Outside of Town

With more people moving outside the suburbs and to rural areas right outside of urban centers, there is a big call for delivery services outside the traditional delivery boundaries.

Becky's house is eight miles outside of Alva, Oklahoma (population 4,900). She would gladly pay extra for an occasional pizza delivery, especially on weekends. Her cousin Matt Achemire lives just outside of Norman, Oklahoma, part of the Oklahoma City metro area (population 1,300,000), in a rural area with many houses on small acreages. He can't get pizza or any other deliveries out there. So, he'll order a pizza to be delivered to the furthest place he can, the stop sign at the end of the country road. Then he goes there to wait for the pizza, rather than drive into town.

With more and more population shifting out of the suburbs because of the ability to do their work from anywhere, delivery services to match make a lot of sense. It's not just fast food. It's also groceries, errand services, and office or household supplies.

Build a Lending Tree–Style Market for Everything

One business idea that could be built from anywhere also uses the any-where, anywhen approach to buying. Take the idea of a Lending Tree–style marketplace, and apply it to any other service. Every customer can identify with the Lending Tree slogan, "When banks compete, you win!" The same could be applied to insurance, legal services, accounting, web design, or many other services.

This idea popped up when C.C. Chapman requested a referral on Twitter. C.C. asked:

> Anyone know a Lending Tree equivalent for home-owner insur-ance? I'm looking for U.S.-based home insurance. I have zero brand loyalty to who I currently have so I figured I'd look around.

The name Lending Tree has become associated with this kind of simple, competitive market space for services.

Buy Global Items to Resell in Local Markets

The same technology that lets professionals do their work from any location also breaks down the former global barriers to trade by small producers. For people and businesses with international experience, there is a market for importing hand crafts. Those who have spent significant time in a different country and returned home have a unique perspective on items that could be good sellers. To learn more about the challenges and regulations, talk with others who are currently successfully importing from the developing world.

Kristen Evans runs Salvatierra[12] importing crafts from Bolivia to the United States. She's succeeding in spite of increasing political difficulties and the constant battles of daily life of her suppliers. She's also found another business sourcing from Bolivia to cooperate with.

Buy Local Items to Resell in Larger Markets

The flip side of taking global items into local markets is taking a local resource into a larger market. Every business has knowledge of some local sources of valuable items. Landfills, garage sales, auctions, local manufacturers, local retailers, or local farmers can be sources of overstocks, scraps, or byproducts.

Businesses can add some value by cleaning, researching, matching, or improving those items. Lots of antiques and collectibles gain in value when the seller does the research and cleans up the items. Clothing resale items gain in value when they are cleaned, matched into outfits, and displayed nicely.

It could be something as simple as buying local garden produce to resell in big city farmers' markets. (This style of "truck farming" has been around forever, in some regions.)

The larger market could be a larger city, an online marketplace, or larger stores. National companies can take advantage of their existing distribution chains to move new items from place to place.

Be a Tour Guide in Online Worlds

As the anywhere, anywhen online world expands, more people need some training or support to understand virtual worlds. That opens up an opportunity for people to offer guided tours online.

"If you've heard of Second Life or World of Warcraft, but didn't know how to begin or where to go or what to do, why not let a real person act as tour guide and show you around?" That's the idea of this business.

As more businesses use virtual worlds for training and events, there will be more opportunity for this kind of tour guide. As every new virtual world opens, brands and businesses are eager to know how to best use them for marketing.

Because many virtual worlds target teens and children, concerned parents are another likely market. This is a business that can operate from any-where where there is web access.

Rule 5: Treat Customers Like Community

Treating customers like community includes responding to their needs, whether that is the need for *less* training or a market that sorely needs attention.

Coach People to Jumping-Off Points

Sometimes, all customers need is someone to show them the basics and get them started. This is especially true for software packages or systems, where the professional users just need a small amount of help to get over the ini-tial learning curve. Online help and documentation don't work as well as personal help. This is an opportunity for brands to offer an exceptional ser-vice for customers, and for coaches and consultants to add a new offering to their portfolio.

After customers get to a jumping off point, they can often manage from there. One- or two-hour sessions with a knowledgeable coach may be all it takes to get to that jumping-off point.

Target the Rural Market

Small towns and rural areas make great target markets. The small town market is a smaller market, but radically underserved. This includes online banking, business coaching, accounting, and business signs, which could all be targeted specifically to rural and small town markets.

Dana Wallert[13] targets the small towns around Lawrence, Kansas, for her virtual assistant and website design business. Wallert says she has better luck marketing in the small towns because there is almost no competition.

When she tries to market inside relatively big Lawrence, Kansas (population 87,000 and center of a metropolitan statistical area), she faces much more competition and has trouble breaking through. Farmers Only[14] targets rural residents for their dating site, and Small Farm Central[15] offers websites designed by farmers, for farmers.

Rule 6: Be Proud of Being Small

Being big is no longer an automatic advantage when winning customers. The preference for small businesses is most evident in the food industry.

Organic Food Is Best from Small Farms

To American consumers, it seems that small farms and small food producers are best. A wave of public awareness and documentaries have made people more wary of mega-large food production and processing. Food-borne illnesses have made headlines from huge commercial production centers and from imported foods. That leaves a big opportunity in small food production. Small businesses and large brands can create profits through small and organic production with premium prices.

Organic production isn't easy, and farmers that are profitable with current production methods are reluctant to convert to the more complex and unreliable systems. It involves some gambling, as some crops become more dependent on weather or susceptible to pests under organic systems. It's also difficult for small producers to find markets, opening more opportunity in distribution and accumulating production from several small operators.

Opportunities also exist outside of farming and production. Restaurants, cafes, food markets, and food processors can all add profitable lines to small or large businesses.

Rule 7: Build Local Connections

The local movement is much more than "shop local." Consumers now prefer local products across all categories. Local can mean a wide range of local connections. Brands can be creative in finding and strengthening their local appeal.

Local-Pride Clothing Shows Off Local Ties

People are used to wearing clothes supporting their favorite sports teams. To build local ties, a business could take that further and create clothing that promotes local pride. This works for small towns, suburbs, and urban neighborhoods.

Neighborhoodies is doing this in New York City. Rather than generic "I love NY" slogans, the company prints designs with "Bed Stuy" for the Bedford-Stuyvesant neighborhood in Brooklyn, for example. It has branched out considerably from that original concept, but still offers neighborhood-pride items.[16]

This idea has been used as far away as Windhoek, Namibia, in Africa. Local women created designs featuring neighborhoods and townships around Namibia. The items sell well with locals and also with tourists eager for a more local connection.[17]

Local Jewelry Creates More Subtle Local Pride

What works for local-pride clothing can also work for jewelry. State of Mine[18] uses state shapes with stones marking hometowns. They do designs for places all across the United States.

A more local example comes from Cape Cod. Jewelry designer Angela Feltman arbitrarily called one bracelet she made "The Cape Cod," and customers kept asking for its significance to the cape. She decided to make a bracelet that really symbolized the towns of the cape. She also donates part of her profits to local schools. Soon, she was getting requests for nearby areas, from Connecticut and Rhode Island.[19] She had accidentally created a new business, built on local ties.

Turn Local Photos into Local Art

Photos of a spectacular sunset over a beach are not hard to find. But a local sunset is a source of local pride, and a photo of a local sunset will outsell a sunset from anywhere else. Local photo products work well in areas with tourists, college students, or other part-time residents, as well as selling to locals.

It doesn't have to be the best photo. What it does have to be is identifiable as local either by landmark or labeling. The product might be a postcard or a poster or even on fabric. What matters is the local connection.[20] Brands and national companies can build local ties by featuring local photos in as many ways as possible. Chesapeake Energy ran a media campaign promoting their local connections featuring the stories and photos of local people in the towns where they have operations.

Personalize Local Photo Postcards with Real People

Photo postcards have been a local souvenir for more than 100 years. Now, it's possible to customize local photo postcards by adding a personal picture of the buyer to photos of local landmarks. For example, an action photo of a local rodeo can be printed alongside the tourist's own photo, taken by the vending machine itself. German company Cosmocard makes this easy with free-standing vending machines. At their website, example postcards show smiling visitors in the center, surrounded by stunning photos of buildings in Munich, or underneath an action picture of a ski jumper in the Alps.[21]

Any small business could set up one of these machines at an event or festival or in a tourist area. Brands have an opportunity to sponsor these kind of souvenirs from factory tours, branded events, or from special purchases.

Cater to Local Outdoor Sports

The fastest growing spectator sport in the U.S. is bird watching, according to Jack Schultz, rural economic development expert. That is followed up with geocaching, biking, hiking, and extreme water sports.[22] Living next to a terrific birding site, the Great Salt Plains National Wildlife Refuge, Becky has seen an increase in the number of birders traveling the area.

Geocaching involves using GPS signals to find hidden caches in parks and other outdoor locations. The caches are left by other enthusiasts, who post the coordinates online. Each person who finds a cache records her visit in the journal inside the cache and exchanges a trinket she's brought with her for one in the cache. Now that most smartphones include GPS tracking, geocaching is growing.

Although most of the wildlife watching is in rural areas, urban areas have pockets of parks, botanical gardens, and other green spaces. Biking and geocaching are especially adaptable to urban green areas.

Local Food Trend

Probably the largest of all local trends is local food. Local food producers of all kinds should capitalize on this opportunity.

Local food trends took 5 out of the top 20 spots in a 2011 National Restaurant Association survey of chefs. Those five local food trends were locally grown produce, local meats, hyperlocal restaurants with their own gardens, farm-branded ingredients, and local beer and wine.[23] Any business that serves food can seek out local producers to buy from. Producers can focus on local markets, and develop methods to go direct to consumers or consumer groups. Every business that provides local foods should promote it prominently in marketing and labeling.

An Ohio State University study observed that people shopping for local foods were knowingly spending almost twice as much for local produce as for the usual trucked-in produce.[24] Another study from Penn State found that restaurant customers will purchase more of items made with local ingredients when they are priced slightly higher than those with non-local ingredients. The items had to both be labeled as local and priced slightly higher than the regular menu items to gain the increase in sales.[25]

Afterword

The Small Town Rules

Here are all seven of the Small Town Rules, put together for review and for easy sharing with others. Because of the major shifts in the economy, technology and society, all business is now forced to play by rules that small town businesses find familiar. All business is like a small town now that every customer can talk directly to every other customer, people listen more to what customers say about a company than they listen to advertising, and people need to have to have multiple jobs to support their families. The individual human voice is now valued over corporate mission statements, people are banding together into small communities online, and local concerns are outweighing national ones. It's just like a small town, and all business has to adapt to these rules. Small town businesses provide the best model for playing by these rules.

The Change in the Economy

There are big parallels in the national economic transition and the transitions in the rural economy over the last 100 years. Small towns have dealt with limited resources, tight lending, and scarce jobs for a long time now.

Rule 1: Plan for zero. There will be tough years ahead.

The corollaries:

1. **Question assumptions.** Believing the prevailing view can be deadly. No matter how stable the current situation seems to be, change can happen. This is often the hardest rule to follow,

because business people are too close to their own assumptions to see what they are.

2. **Know there are seasons and cycles, and plan ahead.** Know the planting times and the harvesting times. Expect there to be a winter dead time in every type of business.

3. **Invest long term in the future.** Those zero years are coming, even when everything seems to be going well. Hold some stockpiles in reserve. During the up years, set aside some for the future and use some profits to make smart investments in the business.

Rule 2: Spend creative brainpower before spending dollars. Remember, too much money can make you stupid.

The corollaries:

1. **Conserve.** Make being frugal a way of life.

2. **Be creative in financing.** Instead of seeking more financial resources, seek more creative solutions. Forget traditional lending sources like banks when there are so many additional ways to find money to grow a business.

3. **Be creative in finding a workforce.** Train a staff locally or find online contingent professionals anywhere in the world that have the needed skills.

4. **Being creative means doing whatever it takes.** Resiliency has always been the hallmark of a successful entrepreneur.

Rule 3: Multiply lines of income to diversify your risk. Don't just count on one way to earn a living.

The corollaries:

1. **Start your own business, at least on the side.** Every person now needs a backup plan. Individuals can explore interests on the side that may become an income-generating opportunity if they lose their job. Brands can consider brand extensions that help diversify the risk.

2. **Manage multiple lines of income.** Find common themes or consolidate opportunities. Find complementary ways to make money that prosper in different economic cycles.

3. **Focus on managing time.** With multiple businesses or income streams, time management and focus become critical for success.

4. **Build one opportunity at a time.** Target one at a time until it is ready to fit in with other projects in the portfolio or until employees can be hired to execute the daily business tasks.

5. **Diversify online.** Extend your company by selling expertise about your business.

The Change in Technology

The transition in technology also pushes all businesses toward small town rules. Geographic advantage has disappeared, and community now means online just as much as offline.

Rule 4: Work anywhere, anywhen through technology. There now is the freedom and responsibility to work outside traditional boundaries.

The corollaries:

1. **Take advantage of broadband.** Fast Internet access is the one utility that is now required for any small business anywhere.

2. **"Anywhen" makes time-shifting as valuable as work-shifting.** Serving customers across the world is now a 24/7 requirement.

3. **Be location independent.** Any small business owner can now live and work where he wants. Time and place are flexible. Any entrepreneur can select the location that best suits his lifestyle, business, family, or preferences. Geography is no longer the barrier to distribution.

4. **Use digital distribution to extend your reach.** Digital distribution is becoming too cheap to measure, allowing businesses to distribute information widely at low cost.

5. **Forget outsourcing, think rural sourcing.** Because a workforce can be anywhere, businesses can reduce costs by using resources that are in more affordable areas of the country.

Rule 5: Treat customers like community. Because they now can talk to each other, they really are like a small town.

The corollaries:

1. **Treat customer service as though it's all you've got.** Product advantages come and go, but giving great customer service secures loyalty. Treat all customers as individuals, and respect their preferences as much as possible.

2. **Use social tools to connect with customers.** With social media, customer service has become the new marketing channel and the small business' only competitive advantage.

The Change in Society

The local movement is pushing a transition in society, one that looks a lot like a small town. The renewed interest in healthy neighborhoods, shopping local and supporting small businesses brings every company back to a small town environment. With public trust and global supply chains stressed, small is back as an alternative in business.

Rule 6: Be proud of being small. This is where the opportunities are in the next decade.

The corollaries:

1. **Build community, be involved.** Come down from the balcony and join the crowd. Let go of the idea of broadcasting one message to a uniform audience. Start making connections with people as individuals to build community. That starts with being friendly, building for the long term, sharing meals, being honest, watching out for others, being helpful, valuing neighbors, getting involved, playing together, having chance encounters, letting others step up and lead, and celebrating together.

2. **Network to build power and accomplish goals.** Beyond building networks of customers, businesses and brands have the opportunity to build a stronger community through local networking, leadership, economic development, workforce development, government, and community groups. Besides local efforts, businesses and brands can take these projects online.

3. **The antidote for the negatives.** Each small community comes with downsides. The answer to most is better communication and openness.

4. **Move past connecting to build relationships.** Customer-relationship management is more than a category of software, it's a way of doing business following the small town rules. Treat people as more than just an email address, build stronger connections, connect in multiple ways, focus attention on the right people, and use the right tools to maintain this as the business grows.

5. **Build community within your customers.** Businesses and brands now have an opportunity to extend the same methods of building community to their customers.

6. **Keep your business small.** Small can be the right size for a business. Not every business is destined to be the next multinational, and that should not be the only goal.

Rule 7: Build your local connections. It's a competitive advantage.

The corollaries:

1. **Connect with your culture and place.** Every business comes from someplace. Rather than drop that local culture to try to fit a homogeneous national culture, successful businesses and brands can retain their culture. There has never been a better time to flaunt a regional accent.

2. **Use a local story to build engagement.** Every place has a story... or lots of stories. By looking through the eight elements of the local culture, businesses can better understand and start telling the stories that customers will connect with.

3. **Build a shop local campaign.** Now that "shop local" is on the
    mind of every consumer, campaigns and projects can grow tre-
    mendously. Small towns, urban neighborhoods, and national
    brands all have the opportunity to forge local connections that
    matter and build a stronger local economy.

Conclusion

The Small Town Rules come from the wisdom of the best small town
businesses. Successful companies survive hardships, cope with or surpass
geographic limits, and build a community among their customers. The
qualities that make small town businesses great have never gone out of
fashion in small towns. Big businesses and national brands have mostly lost
these qualities, but they can bring them back by applying the Small Town
Rules.

Endnotes

Chapter 1

1. http://www.bloomberg.com/apps/news?pid=newsarchive&sid=aaRlfL4VyFwU&refer=news

2. www.bls.gov/news.release/archives/eci_10302009.htm

3. www.wsws.org/articles/2010/dec2010/fore-d31.shtml
   http://en.wikipedia.org/wiki/Subprime_mortgage_crisis

4. *How the Mighty Fall*, Jim Collins

5. http://money.cnn.com/2010/10/20/news/companies/Fortune_500_fallen_angels.fortune/index.htm

6. www.msnbc.msn.com/id/45206685/ns/business-motley_fool/

7. http://online.wsj.com/article/SB1000142405297020349970457662267408241057 8.html

8. http://articles.cnn.com/2011-02-07/world/china.super.bowl.ad_1_groupon-super-bowl-ad-tv-ad?_s=PM:WORLD

9. www.bp.com/sectiongenericarticle.do?categoryId=9036580&contentId=7067577

10. www.bloomberg.com/news/2011-07-15/bp-oil-still-washing-ashore-one-year-after-end-of-gulf-spill.html

11. http://techcrunch.com/2011/04/12/cisco-to-shut-down-flip-video-business-will-give-pink-slips-to-550-employees/

12. Interview with Sheila Scarborough

13. http://shankman.com/the-best-customer-service-story-ever-told-starring-mortons-steakhouse/

14. *The Worst Hard Time*, Timothy Egan

15. www.fema.gov/news/disaster_totals_annual.fema

16. www.wlfi.com/dpp/news/local/survey-rural-residents-more-prepared-than-urban-residents

17. www.smallbizsurvival.com/2006/12/pov-laura-girty-whats-special-about.html

18. www.smallbizsurvival.com/2007/07/rebuilding-from-total-disaster.html

19. www.smallbizsurvival.com/2007/07/wbs-is-coming-back.html

20. *The Worst Hard Time*, Timothy Egan

21. www.vanguard.com

Winnebago Industries

www.winnebagoind.com/company/about-us/story.php

Chapter 2

1. http://news.bbc.co.uk/2/hi/uk_news/7904621.stm

2. http://econintersect.com/wordpress/?p=1762

3. http://online.wsj.com/article/SB10001424053111904836104576558861943984924.html

4. http://abcnews.go.com/Business/hoarding-hiring-corporations-stockpile-mountain-cash/story?id=10250559

5. www.businessweek.com/investor/content/mar2010/pi20100322_127641.htm

6. www.wellsfargo.com/press/20060815_Money

7. www.theleanstartup.com/

8. www.time.com/time/magazine/article/0,9171,2026914,00.html

9. Data from Analysis of Retail Trends and Taxable Sales for Buffalo, Oklahoma, and Harper County, Oklahoma Cooperative Extension Service, OSU, Nov. 2009

10. *Get Your Business Funded: Creative Methods for Getting the Money You Need*, Steven D. Strauss, John Wiley & Sons, 2011, and *Locavesting: The Revolution in Local Investing and How to Profit From It*, Amy Cortese, John Wiley & Sons, 2011.

11. www.opinno.com/blog/2009/9/7/lessons-to-be-learned-from-over-funded-startups.html

12. http://images.forbes.com/forbesinsights/StudyPDFs/SME_CountryFocusReports.pdf

13. www.blogtalkradio.com/bjmoltz/2011/09/02/episode-141-fabio-rosati-ceo-elance

14. http://en.wikipedia.org/wiki/Pets.com

15. http://en.wikipedia.org/wiki/Ingvar_Kamprad

16. www.businessinsider.com/chart-of-the-day-ad-spending-for-tech-companies-2010-5

17. http://articles.latimes.com/2007/mar/04/opinion/op-gross4

18. www.brisbanetimes.com.au/business/we-grew-too-fast-toyota-20100224-p16b.html

19. www.streetdirectory.com/travel_guide/193747/entrepreneurship/watchmefranchise_reviews_4_franchises_that_expanded_too_fast.html

20. www.inc.com/magazine/20070501/salesmarketing-pricing.html

Viking Range

www.vikingrange.com/consumer/global/content.jsp?id=cat12660022

Chapter 3

1. www.usatoday.com/money/economy/2010-05-13-jobs-gone_N.htm

2. www.cbpp.org/cms/index.cfm?fa=view&id=3252

3. www.dailymail.com/News/NationandWorld/201010121079

4. www.nyu.edu/ccpr/katrina-effect.pdf

5. www.cbpp.org/cms/?fa=view&id=711

6. http://hbswk.hbs.edu/archive/1476.html

7. http://ruralsociology.org/StaticContent/Publications/Ruralrealities/pubs/RuralRealities2-3.pdf

8. www.indiebusinessblog.com/about-those-multiple-streams-of-income/

9. Email interview with Bill Burch

10. Walsh-Sarnecki, Peggy. "Eatery flourishes in middle of Huron Co." Detroit Free Press, July 17, 2011.

11. http://joyfullyjobless.com/blog/2010/01/portfolio-building-italian-style/

12. www.twitter.com/gapingvoid

13. www.twitter.com/ginabee/statuses/8260368778

14. www.jonathanfields.com/blog/body-of-work/

15. www.twitter.com/Timberry/statuses/8260508711

16. Banas, Edward J., and W. Frances Emory. "History and Issues of Distance Learning." *Public Administration Quarterly* 22, no. 3 (Fall98 1998): 365-383. Business Source Premier, EBSCOhost (accessed November 18, 2011)

17. www.smallbizsurvival.com/2010/10/small-town-wedding-planner-dreams-big.html

18. www.teachingsells.com

19. www.uiweb.uidaho.edu/eo/dist1.html

20. www.smallbizsurvival.com/2009/09/pov-laura-beulke.html

21. www.entrepreneur.com/article/219405

22. http://brandfailures.blogspot.com/2006/11/brand-extension-failures-virgin-cola.html

23. http://en.wikipedia.org/wiki/Payphone

24. www.cnbc.com/id/39722773/15_Major_Fast_Food_Failures?slide=17

25. http://brandfailures.blogspot.com/2006/12/other-famous-brand-extension-failures.html

Walmart

http://en.wikipedia.org/wiki/Walmart

http://www2.econ.iastate.edu/faculty/stone/10yrstudy.pdf

Chapter 4

1. The Future of the Telephone, Scientific American, January 10, 1880 http://books.google.com/books?id=-389AQAAIAAJ&lpg=PA16&ots=i7iRGfR2nq&dq=The%20Future%20of%20the%20Telephone%2C%20Scientific%20American%2C%20January%2010%2C%201880&pg=PA16#v=onepage&q=The%20Future%20of%20the%20Telephone,%20Scientific%20American,%20January%2010,%201880&f=false

2. The Box: How the Shipping Container Made the World Smaller and the World Economy Bigger, Marc Levinson, Princeton University Press, 2006. http://press.princeton.edu/chapters/s9383.html

3. www.uphoffonmedia.com/2011/06/27/newspapers-dying-the-demise-of-geographic-exclusivity/

4. The Box: How the Shipping Container Made the World Smaller and the World Economy Bigger, Marc Levinson, Princeton University Press, 2006. http://press.princeton.edu/chapters/s9383.html

5. www.imdb.com/title/tt1365483/

6. http://smallbiztrends.com/2011/08/remote-work-no-longer-a-perk- but-a-business-imperative.html

7. www.dol.gov/wb/media/natldialogue3.htm

8. http://myemail.constantcontact.com/Fail-Fast--Fail-Forward--but-Do-Something.html?soid=1101517808896&aid=rGqHaFL05Pc

9. www.agriculture.com/farm-management/technology/cell-phone-and-smart-phones/smartphones-a-big-trend_325-ar20351

10. *Chicago Tribune*, December 11, 2010

11. www.broadbandmap.gov/download/Broadband%20Availability%20in%20Rural%20vs%20Urban%20Areas%20Dec%202010.pdf

12. Interview with Bill Burch

13. www.chrisbrogan.com/the-anywhen-manifesto/

14. www.awayfind.com/blog/2010/03/making-anywhen-a-possibility/

15. www.twitter.com/#!/gapingvoid/status/157894079643004928

16. http://about.van.fedex.com/access/littleguys

17. www.smallbizsurvival.com/2009/12/5-things-i-learned-when-i-moved-my.html

18. http://livingintok.wordpress.com/

19. www.sturgisdevelopment.com/

20. www.blogtalkradio.com/bjmoltz/2011/09/02/episode-141-fabio-rosati-ceo-elance

21. http://scobleizer.com/2008/01/30/the-big-computer-company-with-no-headquarters/

22. www.blogtalkradio.com/bjmoltz/2011/09/02/episode-141-fabio-rosati-ceo-elance

23. http://money.cnn.com/magazines/fortune/bestcompanies/2011/benefits/telecommuting.html

24. www.crowdspring.com

L.L. Bean

www.llbean.com/customerService/aboutLLBean/images/110408_About-LLB.pdf

Chapter 5

1. Brian Clark quote, telephone interview, Third Tribe, March 10, 2010

2. http://blog.nielsen.com/nielsenwire/consumer/global-advertising-consumers-trust-real-friends-and-virtual-strangers-the-most/

3. www.cluetrain.com

4. www.entrepreneur.com/trends/index.html

5. www.davecarrollmusic.com/ubg/story/

6. http://hbswk.hbs.edu/item/6492.html

7. www.cloutsmiths.com/2011/united-breaks-guitars/

8. www.wired.com/magazine/2011/07/st_essay_rating/

9. http://about.americanexpress.com/news/pr/2011/csbar.aspx

10. *We Are All Weird*, Seth Godin

11. www.zoomerang.com/pr-survey-smb-social-media-adoption/

12. http://sethgodin.typepad.com/seths_blog/2009/07/welcome-to-island-marketing.html

13. http://garyvaynerchuk.com/post/247583674/small-town-rules

14. www.smallbizsurvival.com/2010/03/why-small-town-small-biz-has-advantage.html

15. http://nmlab.com/blog/creating-your-own-small-town-the-social-media-way/

16. www.chrisbrogan.com/wire-up-your-customer-base/

17. www.chrisbrogan.com/cafe-shaped-business/

18. www.smallbizsurvival.com/2009/06/overheard-at-140-character-conference.html

19. www.blogtalkradio.com/bjmoltz

20. http://under30ceo.com/not-your-ordinary-salesman-zappos-tony-hsieh/

21. www.smallbizsurvival.com/2009/05/difference-it-makes.html

22. http://mackcollier.com/dell-social-media/

23. www.sheilasguide.com/2010/12/10/the-most-important-thing-i-saw-at-dells-social-media-listening-command-center/

Grasshopper Mowers

www.grasshoppermower.com/about.php

www.lawnandlandscape.com/Article.aspx?article_id=6651

Chapter 6

1. http://sethgodin.typepad.com/seths_blog/2005/06/small_is_the_ne.html

2. www.sba.gov/advocacy/7495/8420

3. http://waysandmeans.house.gov/UploadedFiles/sullivan_written_testimony_WM_Jan_20.pdf

4. www.extension.iastate.edu/communities/news/ComCon56.html

5. www.time.com/time/specials/2007/article/0,28804,1657256_
1655085_1654848,00.html

6. http://about.americanexpress.com/news/pr/2011/csbar.aspx

7. www.openforum.com/articles/shop-small-resonates-with-local-consumers

8. www.twellow.com/categories/ceos

9. http://localglobe.blogspot.com/2007/03/opencoffee-club-structure-
vs-free-form.html

10. www.sethcall.com/blog/2010/09/30/facebook-api-does-not-care/

11. Email interview with Grant Griffiths, speaker at #massivecamp

12. http://blog.smallbusiness.com/2010/03/16/small-business-web-apps-
at-sxs/

13. http://3blmedia.com/theCSRfeed/Nearly-All-Consumers-Likely-Switch-
Brands-Support-Cause-Holiday-Season

14. http://smartblogs.com/socialmedia/2010/04/06/where-social-media-meets-
cause-marketing/

15. http://ja-nae.net/blog/the-power-of-the-epic-win-and-taking-online-gaming-
offline

16. www.openforum.com/articles/game-on-why-gaming-is-a-crucial-part-of-
your-marketing-strategy

17. Fournier Susan, Lee Lara. *Getting Brand Communities Right.* Harvard Business
Review. April 2009; 87(4):105-111. Available from: Business Source Premier,
Ipswich, MA

18. www.fastcompany.com/1771250/9-ways-to-know-your-community-is-truly-
awesome

19. http://alt.goed.utah.gov/initiatives/clusters/benefits.html

20. www.matr.net/

21. www.companiesandcauses.com/cause-update/premier-wine-imports-pairs-
cause-marketing-with-kosher-wine/

22. www.inc.com/articles/201108/6-reasons-to-keep-your-business-small.html

23. *Rework,* Jason Fried and David Heinemeier Hansson, 2010, Crown Business

24. http://about.fedex.designcdt.com/access/littleguys

25. www.usatoday.com/money/advertising/adtrack/2005-05-23-burger-king_x.
htm

26. http://en.wikipedia.org/wiki/Keurig

27. www.gore.com/en_gb/aboutus/culture/index.html

28. www.npr.org/2011/06/04/136723316/dont-believe-facebook-you-only-have-150-friends

29. www.pbs.org/newshour/bb/business/jan-june10/makingsense_04-28.html

30. Gina Debogovich, Best Buy, Social Architect, Enterprise Customer Care, interview and slides

Longaberger Baskets

www.longaberger.com/companyHistory.aspx

Chapter 7

1. http://www.restaurant.org/pressroom/social-media-releases/release/?page=social_media_whats_hot_2012.cfm

2. http://consumerist.com/2007/10/study-shows-shoppers-will-pay-more-than-necessary-for-fair-trade-goods.html

3. www.hartman-group.com/hartbeat/2008-02-27

4. www.newrules.org/retail/article/new-deal-local-economies

5. www.openforum.com/idea-hub/topics/money/article/buy-local-on-the-rise-in-america-1

6. www.thedailybeast.com/newsweek/2009/12/10/the-vogue-for-local.html

7. www.bcg.com/documents/file84471.pdf

8. http://garyvaynerchuk.com/post/247583674/small-town-rules

9. www.smallbizsurvival.com/2009/09/are-small-towns-part-of-past.html

10. www.soulofthecommunity.org/

11. http://thesilverbarn.wordpress.com/

12. http://kansassampler.org/rce/

13. www.pridedairy.com/

14. www.mapleriverwinery.com/

15. www.nuts.com/about-us/our-story

16. www.iopfda.org/iopfda/files/ccLibraryFiles/Filename/000000000368/ibf_survey_pr%20AMIBA%2001-23-08.pdf

17. http://researchnews.osu.edu/archive/locfood.htm

18. www.hartman-group.com/hartbeat/2008-02-27

19. www.moveyourmoney.info

20. www.facebook.com/Nov.Fifth

21. www.iopfda.org/iopfda/files/ccLibraryFiles/Filename/000000000368/ibf_survey_pr%20AMIBA%2001-23-08.pdf

22. www.livingeconomies.org/netview/resources-and-studies/LFstudies

23. www.newrules.org/retail/news/buy-local-changing-shopping-habits-portland-maine

24. www.newrules.org/retail/news/buy-local-philly

25. www.newrules.org

26. www.thebollard.com/bollard/?p=5927

27. www.newrules.org/retail/article/are-buy-local-campaigns-baseless-sloganeering-smug-elites-our-response

28. www.letsdobusinesstulsa.com/

29. http://news.thomasnet.com/IMT/archives/2009/05/small-independent-business-owners-banding-together-buy-local-campaigns.html?t=recent

30. http://boomtownusa.blogspot.com/2007/01/help-your-neighbors.html

31. www.spenditinescondido.org/

32. http://blog.al.com/live/2009/03/brewton_pharmacist_launches_ho.html

33. www.newrules.org/retail/news/buy-local-philly

34. www.livingeconomies.org/sites/default/files/file/Results%20of%20poll%20of%20TLF%20impact.pdf

35. http://letsdobusinesstulsa.com/news.asp?id=824&newsid=525

36. www.salinaschamber.com/BuyLocal.asp

37. www.smallbizsurvival.com/2011/07/community-volunteers-can-help-save.html

38. www.crackerbarrel.com/about-us/

39. www.crackerbarrel.com/about-us/

40. http://en.wikipedia.org/wiki/Einstein_Bros._Bagels

41. http://walmartstores.com/aboutus/297.aspx

42. www.wholefoodsmarket.com/products/locally-grown/

43. www.groupon.com/now/about

44. https://nextdoor.com/

45. www.dexone.com

46. *Budget Magazine*, October 2011, page 33

Appendix B

1. http://www.marketplace.org/topics/life/new-way-support-local-booksellers
2. www.okbid.org
3. www.sba.gov/content/small-business-innovation-research-program-sbir-0
4. www.smallbizsurvival.com/2009/04/hotter-than-hell-night.html
5. www.robertfulghum.com
6. www.smallbizsurvival.com/2007/09/idea-be-more-than-coach.html
7. www.barcharts.com
8. www.1440mainst.com/
9. www.harveyvilleproject.com/
10. www.grist.org/article/2011-01-14-millennials-not-looking-for-mcmansions-unless-they-have-to-live/
11. www.smallbizsurvival.com/2011/06/want-to-retain-more-youth-offer-them.html
12. www.salvatierraimports.com
13. www.dwofficesolutions.com
14. www.farmersonly.com
15. www.smallfarmcentral.com/
16. www.neighborhoodies.com/
17. www.smallbizsurvival.com/2007/05/idea-local-products-outsell-generic.html
18. www.stateofmine.com
19. www.wickedlocal.com/barnstable/homepage/x96463945
20. http://blogs.photopreneur.com/marketing-local/
21. www.cosmoproducts.de/en/home/home.html
22. www.boomtowninstitute.com/Newsletters/20080108.html
23. www.nrn.com/article/chefs-predict-biggest-trends-2011
24. http://researchnews.osu.edu/archive/locfood.htm
25. www.sciencedaily.com/releases/2010/10/101026111733.htm

Index

Z

YOUTUBE *for* BUSINESS
Second Edition
Online Video Marketing for Any Business
MICHAEL MILLER

INTERNET MARKETING START to FINISH
Drive Measurable, Repeatable Online Sales with Search Marketing, Usability, CRM, and Analytics
CATHERINE JUON, DUNRIE GREILING & CATHERINE BUERKLE

CONTENT MARKETING
Think Like a Publisher—How to Use Content to Market Online and in Social Media
REBECCA LIEB

FACEBOOK MARKETING
THIRD EDITION
Leveraging Facebook's Features for Your Marketing Campaigns
BRIAN CARTER · JUSTIN LEVY

SOCIAL MEDIA ROI
Managing and Measuring Social Media Efforts in Your Organization
OLIVIER BLANCHARD

Biz-Tech Series

Straightforward Strategies and Tactics for Business Today

The **Que Biz-Tech series** designed for the legions of small-medium business owners, executives and marketers out there trying to come to grips with emerging technologies that can make or break their business. These books help the reader know what's important, what isn't, and provide deep inside know-how for entering the brave new world of business technology, covering topics such as social media, web marketing, mobile marketing, search engine marketing and blogging.

- Straightforward strategies and tactics for companies who are either using or will be using a new technology/product or way of thinking/doing business.

- Written by well-known industry experts in their respective fields — and designed to be an open platform for the author to teach a topic in the way he or she believes the audience will learn best.

- Covers new technologies that companies must embrace to remain competitive in the marketplace and shows them how to maximize those technologies for profit.

Other Titles You May Like

Google+ for Business
Chris Brogan

THE LIKE ECONOMY
HOW BUSINESSES MAKE MONEY WITH FACEBOOK

NO BULLSHIT SOCIAL MEDIA

SMART BUSINESS, SOCIAL BUSINESS
MICHAEL BRITO

Zero to 100,000
GRATTON & GRATTON

Visit **quepublishing.com/biztech** to learn more.

ALWAYS LEARNING   PEARSON

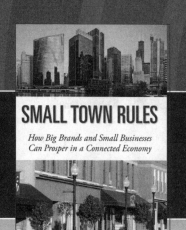

SMALL TOWN RULES

How Big Brands and Small Businesses Can Prosper in a Connected Economy

BARRY J. MOLTZ & BECKY McCRAY

Safari
Books Online

FREE
Online Edition

Your purchase of *Small Town Rules: How Big Brands and Small Businesses Can Prosper in a Connected Economy* includes access to a free online edition for 45 days through the **Safari Books Online** subscription service. Nearly every Que book is available online through **Safari Books Online**, along with thousands of books and videos from publishers such as Addison-Wesley Professional, Cisco Press, Exam Cram, IBM Press, O'Reilly Media, Prentice Hall, Sams, and VMware Press.

Safari Books Online is a digital library providing searchable, on-demand access to thousands of technology, digital media, and professional development books and videos from leading publishers. With one monthly or yearly subscription price, you get unlimited access to learning tools and information on topics including mobile app and software development, tips and tricks on using your favorite gadgets, networking, project management, graphic design, and much more.

Activate your FREE Online Edition at
informit.com/safarifree

STEP 1: Enter the coupon code: NVZYKCB.

STEP 2: New Safari users, complete the brief registration form. Safari subscribers, just log in.

If you have difficulty registering on Safari or accessing the online edition, please e-mail customer-service@safaribooksonline.com